D0524671

# Civil Procedure Simulations

By

**Michael Vitiello**

*University of the Pacific, McGeorge School of Law*

**BRIDGE TO PRACTICE**

WEST®

A Thomson Reuters business

Mat #41166353

610 Opperman Drive
St. Paul, MN 55123
1–800–313–9378

Printed in the United States of America

**ISBN:** 978–0–314–27642–1

*To my wife, Erie.*
*A Civil Procedure professor could not ask*
*for a better wife.*

# ACKNOWLEDGEMENTS

Special thanks go to my acquisitions editors Trina Tinglum and Louis Higgins. The proposal for the Simulation Series was in front of another publisher for several months when I submitted it to West at Trina's suggestion. Within a few days of receiving the proposal, Louis questioned me about the proposal with insight and intensity. My offer to publish the series came within a matter of a few days. I extend my thanks also to my Pacific McGeorge colleagues who have committed to publishing books in the Simulation Series. Their participation is transforming the concept into a series.

I am especially appreciative for the excellent research assistance provided by Pacific McGeorge students Patrick Blood, Ashley Connell, R.J. Cooper and Mariel Covarrubias. I offer my special thanks to McGeorge student Karl Schweikert for not only explaining the Internet and Web to me but also for drafting part of the deposition in Chapter Two, dealing with minimum contacts and the Web. I also wish to thank Pacific McGeorge librarian Michele Finerty for considerable help in locating an array of documents, Faculty Support staff member R.K. Van Every for her help with solving any number of technical problems and for her careful proofreading of the text and teacher's manual, and Faculty Support staff member Wendy Owens for her help.

# ACKNOWLEDGMENTS

# INTRODUCTION

*I. Background Goals*

When I began law school in 1971, my Civil Procedure professor assigned a short pamphlet that consisted of several legal documents. After assigning it, the professor never referred to it again. That was my last exposure to realistic legal documents until I began working during the summer after my second year. I began teaching Civil Procedure in 1977 and for many years watched students struggle with arcane concepts of procedure. In the mid-1990's, I developed a series of simulation exercises in my procedure course.

My simulation worked well for my own pedagogical purposes. But recent developments have made a book like this more important. In 2007, the Carnegie Foundation's *Educating Lawyers: Preparation for the Profession of Law* was published. *Educating Lawyers* recognized that the standard first-year curriculum is good at helping students to think like lawyers and provides sufficient academic knowledge and development. But the report faulted the curriculum for failing to teach law students to act like lawyers. It criticized law schools for the separation of theoretical learning from skills training.

The report compared legal and medical education, which incorporates clinical or experiential learning into students' formal education.[1] The report argued that such an implementation would be beneficial because the purpose of all professional education, legal and otherwise, is to serve in the place of an apprenticeship. The traditional purpose of an apprenticeship is not merely the academic advancement of the new practitioners, but also the practical development of the skills necessary to be proficient.

The timing of *Educating Lawyers* was critical. In the past, other reports like the McCrate Report in the 1980's have urged greater experiential learning but did not have a dramatic impact on legal education. Coming at a time when legal educators have paid more attention to learning theory, *Educating Lawyers* has had an immediate effect. Responding to the Carnegie Report, a number of prominent law schools announced substantial curricular changes to increase experiential learning opportunities for their students. Conferences on implementing the report have proliferated.

A second important factor that, I hope, makes this kind of book timely and valuable is the change in the job market for entry level lawyers. Although the trend began before the economic downturn in 2008, corporate clients of

1. Legal educators use "experiential learning" to mean somewhat different things. For some, it is clinical education. More broadly, however, the term also includes classroom simulation exercises. Classroom exercises have a number of advantages over clinical learning: most importantly, a professor can design material that teaches a fixed set of skills. Whether a student gets a particular set of experiences in a clinical setting may be a matter of chance.

large law firms have resisted paying additional fees for associates. They have challenged one of the traditions of the legal profession, the mentoring of junior lawyers by senior lawyers. That practice is now considered too expensive. That is so not only because of resistance from large clients, but also because, unlike an earlier era, young lawyers no longer make long-term commitments to their firms. Thus, by the time a firm recoups the cost of training a new associate, the now-experienced lawyer moves to a new position. Further, when firms do hire recent graduates, they want new associates to provide "value added" immediately.

During the summer of 2011, the Association of American Law Schools hosted an event in Seattle. The Association advertised the Conference on the Future of the Law School Curriculum in urgent terms: "We are at a pivotal moment in the history of legal education." Forces from inside and outside of the academy are calling for changes in the law school curriculum. One suggested area of change was greater incorporation of experiential learning into the traditional curriculum.

One way in which legal educators can respond to the demand for graduates who can add value to their employers sooner rather than later is by having them develop practical skills from the beginning of their legal careers. Rather than teaching students only abstract concepts, for example, those of us in the academy should teach our students how to apply those concepts in realistic settings.

That is the purpose of this and similar books in West's Simulation Series. This book is designed for students enrolled in a basic Civil Procedure course, usually offered to One L students. My hope is that students will realize why procedural rules matter and why procedure may be far more important than substantive rules in deciding how a case will be resolved.

This book contains a single narrative, a story about a plaintiff who faces publication of a story that will devastate her and destroy her career. You will be called on to make various strategic decisions. For example, where should the plaintiff file her lawsuit? Why does that matter? By the end of the course, I hope that you understand the power that procedure has in deciding real human crises.

*II. Dramatis Personae and the Outline of the Plot*

For many years, John Elliot was a crusading district attorney in Doddville, Connecticut. First, as the County District Attorney, and later as state Attorney General, he pursued corruption at all levels of levels of government. His performance earned him the respect of Governor Ernie Edmunds. Concerned that Elliot might be a formidable gubernatorial opponent, Edmunds appointed Elliot to the state appellate bench.

Elliot's reputation as a crusader inspired many law students. Many of them campaigned for him when he ran for elected office. Once he was on the bench, top law students vied to serve as his law clerks.

One lucky aspirant was Sarah Nobile, a lifelong resident of Doddville. A star student at the Connecticut State University Law School, she accepted a two-year clerkship with the judge in YR-5. While she became close to her mentor, her clerkship was marked by a poor relationship with her fellow clerk, Nathan Loewe, an ambitious young man who graduated from an Ivy League law school where he was the editor-in-chief of its premier law review.

In YR-3, facing re-election to the bench, Judge Elliot decided to resign from the bench at the end of his term. He did not announce his future plans, but many speculated that if Janet Rodman won the up-coming presidential election, she would appoint Elliot to the federal district court or name him to serve as the United States Attorney for the Central District of Connecticut. While he had yet to announce his plans, Elliot seemed upbeat about his options. That would change quickly.

On the morning of June 1, YR-3, the judge's secretary, Rhoda Sheen, was confronted by a group of local law enforcement agents, armed with a search warrant for the judge's chambers. While the lead officer explained that Sheen could not resist compliance with the search warrant, the police had arranged to execute the warrant early in the morning to avoid attention of the public and the media. The police seized the four office computers, including Nobile's and the judge's.

Several days later, Clara Saint-Jean, the local district attorney, notified the judge that a technician for the police found files containing child pornography on two of the computers. One was the judge's and the other was Nobile's.

Despite that, she told him that her office had rejected the recommendation from the police to pursue criminal charges. Although not a friend of the judge's, Saint-Jean respected his work. Further, although her comments were not for the record, she told him that her office was troubled by sloppy police work. She is not sure how members of the force learned about the pornography. She thinks that the police have been working with someone in the judge's chambers who provided information illegally. She also interviewed the judge's secretary after the case was referred to her and learned that the judge and Nobile often left their computers on even when they left the office. Further, they often worked late at night and on weekends, when cleaning staff also had access to the judge's chambers.

Apart from thanking her for the decision not to prosecute and denying his own guilt, Judge Elliot told Saint-Jean that he doubted that Nobile was involved. He knew her well and believed in her integrity. Further, he was sure that she had no interest in child pornography. Because he was convinced that someone had tried to set him up and because the effect on Nobile's career would be devastating, the judge asked Saint-Jean if she would have the search warrant sealed. She agreed to do so.

The judge confided in Nobile about what he learned from Saint-Jean. She was distraught, not only for herself but for the judge. After considerable counseling from the judge, she decided to look for work out of state. Based on her strong record in law school and a strong recommendation from the judge, she received an offer from Breeze and Associates, LLC, a plaintiff's class action firm in Cuomo City, New York. The firm also has an office in Doddville where it has been involved in a major case against Mega Market, Inc., captioned *Karen Foss v. Mega Market, Inc.* Breeze represents a class consisting of women claiming gender discrimination against Mega.

Despite renting an apartment in Cuomo City, Nobile has kept her condominium in Doddville because of her heavy involvement in the *Foss v. Mega Market* litigation. Shortly after she began working at Breeze, she met and fell in love with fellow associate Nick Rossi. They were married on January 1, YR-10. Her heavy schedule allowed her to stay in Cuomo City with her husband only on occasional weekends.

After most of a year at her new job, she received an unsettling phone call from Ms. Sheen while Nobile was working at her office in Cuomo City. Now retired, but still living in Doddville, Sheen explained she received a call from Mike Ridge, who identified himself as an Internet investigative reporter. Ridge told Sheen he was writing a story about a judge who had been able to quash criminal charges for possession of child pornography because of his political influence. He believed Judge Elliot was involved in the case. Sheen told Ridge that there was nothing to the story, but he remained skeptical. Ridge also mentioned Nobile by name and implied that his source identified her as implicated as well. Ridge also hinted that he would be publishing an article making these accusations on his blog, GOTCHA!

Distressed, Nobile did a quick check of Ridge's background. She learned he barely graduated from Connecticut State University's School of Journalism. On his webpage, he bragged about his indifferent record at the University and accused the faculty of being naïve adherents to outmoded ideals of journalism. Those standards, according to Ridge, died along with Edward R. Murrow and Walter Cronkite. Instead, Internet reporters must follow leads quickly and confront the powerful. Erroneously attributing the phrase to Justice Oliver Wendell Holmes, Ridge claims the First Amendment to our Constitution creates a "marketplace of ideas," and, if a story is false, the Internet provides a person an immediate and affordable forum where she can correct falsehoods. Further, his website demonstrated his deep distrust of politicians. It prominently displayed a quotation from Mark Twain, which summarized his creed: "Politicians are America's Criminal Class."

With the hope of stopping the story, which Nobile believed would be defamatory and harmful to her and to the judge, Nobile called Ridge on a cell phone number she found on his webpage. She did not get hold of him immediately, but left a voicemail explaining her need to talk to him. He called back the next day from his office in Doddville. He told her that she was a target of the story but that he was really after the big hypocrite, the judge. He intimated that if she provided sufficient background information about the judge, he would not include her name in the stories.

She begged for some time to consider what to do. She called the judge immediately. He speculated that someone was feeding Ridge information to damage the judge's plans to make a political comeback. He suggested that she contact the U.S. Attorney's office because Ridge's threat seemed to amount to extortion and was probably a violation of federal criminal law. Short of that, they discussed whether she might be able to file an action against Ridge to stop publication of the story.

That is the beginning of the story that you will follow during the course of this book. Each chapter relates to different procedural aspects of this case.

*III. Some Administrative Details*

You have already noticed that I have not included a year but instead have used YR-00, YR-01, YR-02, etc. YR-00 is the year in which you are using the book; YR-01 (year minus one) is last year, YR-02, two years ago, etc. Many case files for courses like Trial Advocacy use a similar system to avoid the texts from becoming obsolete. As a result, where the text indicates a day of a month when an event takes place or papers are filed, the date may take place on a Saturday or Sunday. Courts are obviously closed on weekends. You should ignore that possible basis of attack. Also you will find, as you move from chapter to chapter, that the book does not always follow a consistent time line. Thus, in one chapter, a party filed a document on one date that may be inconsistent with dates in other chapters. You should ignore inconsistent dates from chapter to chapter.

While the case and the documents in this book are fictitious, I have tried to create realistic documents. An important goal of this book is to familiarize you with legal documents and the procedural steps that lawyers take in pursuing cases for their clients. One final observation before you proceed to your first assignment is that you may find what appear to be inconsistencies (for example, in a person's testimony or between accounts by participants in the relevant events) or errors in documents. Facts are often messy; witnesses' accounts differ or one witness may forget or unintentionally or intentionally change her account of important events. Welcome to the practice of law!

# TABLE OF CONTENTS


DEDICATION ---------- iii
ACKNOWLEDGEMENTS ---------- v
INTRODUCTION ---------- vii

**Chapter One. Selecting a Forum** ---------- **1**
I. Introduction ---------- 1
II. The Interview ---------- 1
III. The Relevant Case Law ---------- 4

**Chapter Two. Personal Jurisdiction** ---------- **17**
I. Introduction ---------- 17
II. The Lawsuit: The Summons and Complaint ---------- 18
III. Assuring Adequate Notice: Serving Process ---------- 28
IV. The Defendants' Response ---------- 29
V. The Defendants' Motion ---------- 30
VI. The Factual Record ---------- 33

**Chapter Three. Subject Matter Jurisdiction (Diversity)** ---------- **50**
I. Introduction ---------- 50
II. Diversity ---------- 50
III. Supplemental Jurisdiction ---------- 51
A. Some Study Questions ---------- 51
B. The Amended Complaint ---------- 52
C. Additional Study Questions ---------- 55

**Chapter Four. Subject Matter Jurisdiction (Federal Question) and Removal** ---------- **57**
I. Introduction ---------- 57
II. The Lawsuit: Some Background ---------- 58
III. The Lawsuit: The Complaint[2]2 ---------- 59
IV. The Defendants' Strategy ---------- 62
V. The Defendants' Notice of Removal to Federal Court ---------- 63
VI. Plaintiff's Motion to Remand ---------- 65
VII. The Simulation ---------- 66

**Chapter Five. Venue and Transfer of Venue** ---------- **68**
I. Introduction ---------- 68
II. Venue and Transfer of Venue ---------- 69
III. The Simulation ---------- 71
IV. Relevant Case Law ---------- 73
**Chapter Six. Motion to Dismiss for Failure to State a Claim for Relief** ---------- **76**
I. Introduction ---------- 76
II. Pleading and Motions: Some Background ---------- 76
III. The Lawsuit: The Complaint ---------- 80
IV. The Defendants' Strategy ---------- 83
V. The Simulation Exercise ---------- 83
VI. Connecticut Choice of Law ---------- 86
**Chapter Seven. Discovery** ---------- **96**
I. Introduction ---------- 96
II. Discovery: Some Background ---------- 96
III. The Scope of Discovery ---------- 98
IV. Forms of Discovery ---------- 100
A. Automatic Disclosure ---------- 100
B. Interrogatories ---------- 101
C. Production of Documents ---------- 102
D. Depositions ---------- 103
E. Physical or Mental Examinations ---------- 105
F. Admissions ---------- 106
V. Forms ---------- 107
A. Discovery Plan ---------- 107
B. Sample Interrogatories ---------- 110
C. Requests for Documents ---------- 112
D. Requests for Admissions ---------- 116
**Chapter Eight. Amending the Complaint** ---------- **117**
I. Introduction ---------- 117
II. Learning the Identities of Unknown Parties ---------- 117
A. Relevant Interrogatories ---------- 118
B. The First Deposition ---------- 118
C. Ongoing Discovery ---------- 120
III. The Simulation: Amending the Complaint ---------- 120
IV. The Crazy Quilt or the Relevant Case Law ---------- 121
A. Relying on F.R.C.P. 15(c)(1)(A) ---------- 121
B. Relying on F.R.C.P. 15(c)(1)(C) ---------- 129
**Chapter Nine. Motion to Dismiss for Summary Judgment** ---------- **140**
I. Introduction ---------- 140
II. Summary Judgment Motions: Some Background ---------- 140
III. The Simulation ---------- 145
A. Satisfying F.R.C.P. 56(c) ---------- 145
B. Satisfying F.R.C.P. 56(e) ---------- 151
C. More on Satisfying F.R.C.P. 56(e) ---------- 151
IV. Cases Relevant to Section III. B ---------- 152

# Civil Procedure Simulations

**BRIDGE TO PRACTICE**

# CHAPTER ONE

# SELECTING A FORUM

## I. INTRODUCTION

This exercise introduces you to the legal problem that you will be dealing with throughout your Civil Procedure course. It also gives you an opportunity to interview a client. In doing so, you should be aware of several goals that you should have for your interview. This section reviews those goals. Thereafter, the chapter consists of an assignment that your employer has given you, which requires you to prepare for an interview with your client. In doing so, you will need to review the four cases found at the end of this chapter.

Being a successful lawyer involves more than legal knowledge. Like doctors, lawyers need to develop good "bedside manner." Many clients seek advice of counsel when they are facing extremely difficult circumstances. As a result, they may be emotionally distraught and be in need of comfort. One of your goals will be to develop rapport with your client.

That cannot be your only goal when you meet your client. You have a limited amount of time to accomplish the work required of you. You need to collect relevant factual material. You need to learn whether your client's case meets all of the legally required elements to state a claim for relief. You may have done some background legal research in advance of the interview. But as you learn the facts, you may need to return to the library for additional research.

Before filing suit, an attorney has an obligation to make a reasonable investigation into the factual allegations in the plaintiff's complaint. As you will learn in a number of courses in law school, the term "reasonable" lacks a precise definition and is often determined on a case-by-case basis. As you will see in this case, time is of the essence. Your ability to do an extensive factual inquiry may destroy your chances of avoiding the harm that your client most fears. In many cases, another goal during the first interview with the client is assessing her credibility. In a case where you have so little time to investigate before you must file the action, that assessment becomes all the more important when the question is whether you have fulfilled your obligation to do a reasonable investigation.

## II. THE INTERVIEW

Assume that you are a junior associate in Connell and Associates, LLP, a law firm located in Cuomo City, New York. The senior partner called you late last evening and told you that s/he received a frantic call from Sarah Nobile, a young woman, whom the partner says the firm is going to represent. After giving you a brief factual overview of Ms. Nobile's legal problems, the partner told you to do some research on the torts of defamation and invasion of privacy in New York and Connecticut. S/he told you that you needed to be prepared to brief the partner on a number of legal issues in connection with a meeting that you and the partner would be having the next morning.

Dutifully, you spent a good part of the night researching the law of New York and Connecticut. Despite reading numerous cases, you have found four cases attached below and edited them for the partner. Those cases give a good summary of the relevant legal rules that may govern the firm's new client's case. The partner also told you that you should prepare to interview Ms. Nobile at the meeting scheduled for 9:00 A.M.

Although you were a little groggy when the partner called, you scribbled some notes. You think that they summarize accurately what the partner told you about Ms. Nobile. You will certainly want to do a more thorough follow-up during the interview.

Here are the facts that you learned last night: about a year ago, Ms. Nobile moved to Cuomo City to take a job at Breeze and Associates, a well-known boutique plaintiffs' class action firm. She has an apartment in Cuomo City but still spends a lot of time in Doddville, Connecticut, where she went to law school and used to work for a prominent judge on the Connecticut Court of Appeals. You recognize the name of the judge, John Elliot, and vaguely remember some details about the judge.

The partner also tells you that Ms. Nobile recently learned that an Internet journalist Mike Ridge intends to publish a story that will name her and Judge Elliot as having been the target of a criminal investigation in YR-03. Ridge claims that he has proof that the judge was able use his political connections to quash criminal charges against him and Ms. Nobile for possession of child pornography. Ms. Nobile explains that three years ago, police raided the judge's chambers and found pornography on two of the office computers. She claims that someone else must have had access to her computer and that she never went to such a site and would never have downloaded such vile material. She suspects her former co-clerk, a man named Nathan Loewe. He did not get along well with the judge and resented her close relationship with the judge.

The partner also tells you that Ms. Nobile fears that the story will destroy the judge's attempt to make a political comeback. Ms. Nobile also knows that, if the story is published, she may lose her job. Finally, the partner tells you that Mr. Ridge seems more interested in "nailing" the judge than he does in humiliating Ms. Nobile; despite that, Ridge has made clear that he will name her in his story and will do so in the very near future.

Ms. Nobile will be in class. Consider any additional questions that you need to ask her.

To prepare for the conference with the partner and the interview with Ms. Nobile, consider the following questions:

1. What is the obvious practical problem that you face given that the harm feared by Ms. Nobile will occur if you do not stop Mr. Ridge immediately? How do the Federal Rules of Civil Procedure deal with the problem that Ms. Nobile faces? Review F.R.C.P. 65.

2. Does Ms. Nobile have a claim for relief against Mr. Ridge? Assume that the plausible rights of action are libel and invasion of privacy. Examine the two New York cases, *Freihofer v. Hearst Corp.* and *Chapadeau v. Utica Observer–Dispatch*, and the two Connecticut cases, *Goodrich v. Waterbury Republican–American, Inc.*, and *Knize v. Knize,* attached below. You are licensed in New York and are familiar with the local courts. As a result, you would prefer to file the action in New York. Are Ms. Nobile's chances of getting relief better under New York or Connecticut substantive law? If you file in a New York court, will New York substantive law necessarily apply?

3. Apart from your personal preference to file the action in a court in New York, what kinds of considerations may influence a person's decision to file in one state as opposed to another state? New York and Connecticut are not far apart (although some areas of New York, like Buffalo, are more than 400 hundred miles from Connecticut). Further, some rural areas of New York are quite different culturally from more urban states like Connecticut. To make the point more clearly, what if a plaintiff from Mississippi was choosing whether to sue a defendant from New York in Mississippi or New York? If the plaintiff can meet all of the requirements to file suit (including personal jurisdiction, venue and the like), can you see practical reasons why she may want to sue in one state or the other?

4. Can Ms. Nobile file her action in a federal court as opposed to a state court? Examine 28 U.S.C § 1332. Can you think of any reasons to choose a federal, rather than a state, court? In this case, Mr. Ridge has yet to publish the story. In light of that fact, if you file in federal court on behalf of Ms. Nobile based on § 1332, will you be able to meet the jurisdictional amount? Can you think of other reasons why a person may want to choose federal over state or vice versa?[1]

5. When the senior partner told you about this case, s/he indicated that Ms. Nobile suspects that Mr. Ridge may have had help in getting information about Ms. Nobile. Would it make sense to join any additional defendants in the action? Can you anticipate any advantages and disadvantages with adding other parties?

6. If you decide to file the action in New York, you will need to research New York law to see how you can commence a lawsuit and how to serve a defendant with the relevant legal papers. If the defendant is an out-of-state resident, you will need to determine what the state's "long-arm" statute provides. Assume that New York's long-arm statute allows you to file the action against Mr. Ridge, will the court have personal jurisdiction over the defendant? Why may there be a problem?

1. Each state has at least one federal district. Some, like California and New York, have four districts. Those courts are usually located in larger cities. Counties in each state usually have a courthouse in the county seat. As a result, in many states, courts are likely to be located in far more rural areas than are federal courts.

7. Can you think of any other issues that you may want to discuss with the members of the firm?

All of the questions above relate to the decision about where to file a lawsuit. The plaintiff's lawyer is engaged in forum shopping, whereby s/he must decide whether the court is a proper forum. Often, a plaintiff may choose between state or federal court or between courts in different states. At this point in your legal studies, your professor does not expect you to be able to give definitive answers to the previous questions. But those questions should help you to start thinking about issues relating to selecting the best forum for your client.

# III. THE RELEVANT CASE LAW

## FREIHOFER v. HEARST CORPORATION

480 N.E. 2d 349 (N.Y. Ct. App. 1985)

KASSAL, JUDGE.

Does the publication by a newspaper of an article relating to the details of court files in matrimonial proceedings rendered confidential by Domestic Relations Law § 235, give rise to a cause of action for (a) invasion of privacy under Civil Rights Laws §§ 50 * * *?

This action was brought to recover damages resulting from the publication of three newspaper articles, relating to a matrimonial action between plaintiff and his wife. The complaint alleges that the publications were in violation of Domestic Relations Law § 235(1), which provides in respect to matrimonial actions: "An officer of the court * * * or his clerk, either before or after the termination of the suit, shall not permit a copy of any of the pleadings, affidavits * * * or testimony, or any examination or perusal thereof, to be taken by any other person than a party, or the attorney or counsel of a party, except by order of the court."

The three news articles were published in defendant's *The Times Union* on September 26 and December 31, 1982 and in the *Knickerbocker News* on December 31, 1982. The publications reported some of the marital difficulties experienced by plaintiff, one of the principals of the Charles Freihofer Baking Company, a well-known company engaged in the sale of baked goods and associated products for more than 70 years. It is undisputed that the factual content of the articles was obtained from confidential court records. The September 26th article, captioned "Freihofer's Fighting Over the Dough," quoted extensively from affidavits filed in the marital suit in connection with a pending application for exclusive occupancy of the marital residence, an estate in Loudonville, in which the Freihofers had lived during their 10–year marriage. Included in the article were charges and countercharges of mental and physical cruelty and adultery which formed the legal basis for the matrimonial action.

Following the first publication, plaintiff's attorneys wrote to *The Times Union* on October 1, 1982, objecting to the publication of the story and the use of plaintiff's photograph, advising as to "the statutory confidentiality protecting court papers of this kind" and demanding that there be no further publication or commentary about "the marital discord" between the parties. Nevertheless, on December 31, 1982, *The Times Union* published its second news story, covering the Appellate Division's reversal of Special Term's order, which had ordered the wife to leave the marital abode and set a hearing on the issue of temporary custody of their son. On the same day, the Knickerbocker News carried a similar story that a hearing had been directed to determine exclusive possession of the Loudonville home and referring to the charges and countercharges of "abusive and cruel behavior."

Defendant admits having reviewed court records in connection with the preparation of the news articles. However, it denies any violation of Domestic Relations Law § 235, contending that papers and pleadings in court actions, including matrimonial suits, are readily available for inspection at the county clerk's office and the Appellate Division; such an examination is "not an uncommon practice" in the preparation of a news story; and the news media "regularly" reports with respect to matrimonial proceedings which affect the public interest. In addition, the motion was argued in open court and the proceedings were available to the public, including the press. Furthermore, it contends it did exercise discretion by omitting from publication many of the personal details relating to the marital action, contained in filed court papers, which would have subjected the parties to unnecessary ridicule or embarrassment and that the stories merely reported the facts, without any sensationalism. Defendant urges that, notwithstanding the cloak of confidentiality under Domestic Relations Law § 235(1), it did not violate the statute, which is directed only to officers and clerks of the court and, in any event, considering the prominence of the Freihofer family in the Albany area and the extensive television and newspaper advertising to promote the Freihofer name, the articles did deal with matters of legitimate public interest and concern.

Plaintiff, on the other hand, alleges that the publications were improperly based upon examination of matrimonial court records. As a result, he says he suffered extreme emotional and physical distress, which affected his business and private relationships, diminished his standing in the community, subjected him to public scorn and ridicule and impaired his social life. The complaint for compensatory and exemplary damages contains [3 causes of action for invasion of privacy under Civil Rights Law §§ 50 and 51] * * *.

* * * Special Term * * * denied defendant's motion for summary judgment to dismiss the first, fifth and ninth causes of action for violation of Civil Rights Law §§ 50 and 51, and plaintiff's cross motion for summary judgment, concluding that there was an issue as to whether the publication of the articles and use of plaintiff's name and photograph were of legitimate concern to the public.

The Appellate Division unanimously affirmed. * * * As to those causes of action predicated upon Civil Rights Law §§ 50 and 51, it agreed with Special Term that there were factual issues, as to whether the articles were newsworthy and of public interest or were published merely to increase circulation, which, it held, would violate the statute.

We disagree and, accordingly, modify to dismiss the first, fifth and ninth causes of action under the Civil Rights Law.

Sections 50 and 51 of the Civil Rights Law make actionable the use of one's "name, portrait or picture" for advertising or trade purposes, without securing the person's consent. The statute created a limited right of privacy, which had not existed prior to the enactment * * * In *Roberson*, it was held that any protection to be accorded for the unauthorized use of one's name or photograph was a matter for the Legislature and could not be created by judicial pronouncement. The legislative response came the following year, with the enactment of Civil Rights Law §§ 50 and 51 (L. 1903, ch. 132, §§ 1, 2).

We have in the past recognized that, in this State, there is no common-law right of privacy and the only available remedy is that created by Civil Rights Law §§ 50 and 51. * * * In these cases, we took cognizance of the limited scope of the statute as granting protection only to the extent of affording a remedy for commercial exploitation of an individual's name, portrait or picture, without written consent.

Thus, the central issue in any case involving an alleged appropriation of plaintiff's name, portrait or picture is whether the use by defendant was primarily for trade or advertising purposes within the meaning of the statute. While the statute does not furnish any definition of trade or advertising purposes, it has been held that the protection afforded by this statute to individuals does not apply to the publication of newsworthy matters or events. The "newsworthiness exception" has long been recognized in this State. * * *

Applying the statute here, both Special Term and the Appellate Division were of the view that a factual issue existed as to whether the primary purpose underlying the publications was to report on a news event or matter of public interest or merely to promote circulation. To the contrary, the critical factor as to the statutory protection under Civil Rights Law § 51, is the content of the published article in terms of whether it is newsworthy, which is a question of law, and not the defendant's motive to increase circulation. [But as the court has held previously] * * *: "The fact that the defendant may have included this item in its column solely or primarily to increase the circulation of its magazine and therefore its profits * * * does not mean that the defendant has used plaintiff's picture for trade purposes within the meaning of the statute. Indeed, most publications seek to increase their circulation and also their profits. It is the content of the article and not the defendant's motive or primary motive to increase circulation which determines whether it is a newsworthy item, as opposed to a trade usage, under the Civil Rights Law * * *."

Plaintiff argues that the publication of matrimonial court files, standing alone, amounts to an invasion of privacy, inasmuch as Domestic Relations Law § 235 prohibits such disclosure by court personnel. This contention, however, overlooks the fact that, in the absence of further legislation, there is no independent right to such relief. The Legislature has not established a cause of action for violation of Domestic Relations Law § 235. In any event, no claim to that effect has been interposed here.

Moreover, in light of our holding [elsewhere] * * * plaintiff may not do so. * * * We did recognize, however, that the constitutional right of the press to publish the allegations in a matrimonial suit, obtained from court files without permission, could not be impinged upon except that liability would be imposed for defamatory publication. * * *

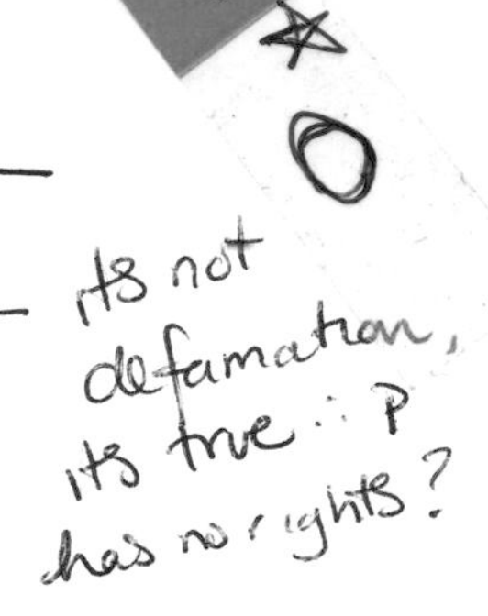

In [the case before the court] * * *, there is no claim for defamation or that the content of the articles is untruthful. Domestic Relations Law § 235 does not provide for an independent cause of action against those who publish or disseminate matter relating to a matrimonial action obtained in violation of the statute. * * *

## CHAPADEAU v. UTICA OBSERVER–DISPATCH, INC.

341 N.E.2d 569 (N.Y. 1975)

WACHTLER, JUDGE.

This appeal concerns the granting of summary judgment in favor of the defendant in a defamation action. Appellant, Chapadeau, is a public school teacher who was arrested in Utica on June 10, 1971 and charged with criminal possession of a hypodermic instrument and criminal possession of a dangerous drug, heroin, in the fourth degree. The next day, respondent's newspaper, The Utica Observer–Dispatch, reported Chapadeau's arrest in an article which also related that two Herkimer men had been arrested on misdemeanor drug charges. After reporting the three arrests the newspaper account went on to state that, "The trio was part of a group at a party in Brookwood Park where they were arrested. Drugs and beer were found at the party, police charge." Appellant claims that the quoted sentences which were false and maliciously published, libeled him. The newspaper admitted the falsity of those sentences but contended that in its entirety the article was a fair and true report and moved for summary judgment.

The trial court denied the motion but was subsequently reversed. The Appellate Division held that in light of Chapadeau's occupation and the nature of the crime his arrest was a matter of public interest and therefore qualifiedly privileged. * * * [T]he Appellate Division concluded that the communication was privileged absent malice and the mere showing of defendant's failure to discover and correct the error was insufficient to warrant a trial on the issue of malice.

On appeal the appellant contends that the Appellate Division order must be overturned because the constitutional privilege with respect to matters of public interest which had been mandated by [the United States Supreme Court was subsequently abandoned by that Court.] Thus, the principal issue is on what basis, subject to the limitations enunciated [by the United States Supreme Court] may a publisher of defamatory falsehoods about a private individual be held liable. We agree with the appellant that liability for publishing matters of public interest should be governed by some sort of fault standard, nevertheless, we conclude that in this case summary judgment was proper.

Prior to the landmark decision in New York Times Co. v. Sullivan, * * * the constitutional protections embodied in the First Amendment did not extend to defamatory statements. However, in the New York Times case, the Supreme Court brought the law of libel within the ambit of constitutional protection by holding that a public official could not recover for a defamatory statement about his official conduct in the absence of proof of malice. Although this constitutional privilege was limited in applicability to public officials, it was soon greatly expanded to include lower echelon officials * * * candidates for public office * * * and plaintiffs classified as public figures. * * *

[The court discussed how the United States Supreme Court initially extended free speech protections even in cases involving private individuals who became involved involuntarily in public controversies. It then discussed how the Court cut back on the First Amendment protection in such cases.] The [Supreme Court] * * * felt that private individuals are more vulnerable because they lack a forum to rebut the false statements and that they are more deserving of recovery because they have not thrust themselves into the vortex of public controversy. Consequently, the court concluded that the States should be accorded 'substantial latitude' in fashioning a remedy based on fault.

However, lest the pendulum swing back too far, the court set forth certain limitations. First, the court abolished the concept of strict liability which had existed at common law * * * and directed that there be no liability without fault * * * Secondly, the doctrine of presumed damages which governed at common law was eliminated and recovery restricted to compensation for actual injury. Lastly, the award of punitive damages was precluded, except on a showing of knowledge of falsity or reckless disregard for the truth. * * *

We now hold that within the limits imposed by the Supreme Court where the content of the article is arguably within the sphere of legitimate public concern, which is reasonably related to matters warranting public exposition, the party defamed may recover; however, to warrant such recovery he must establish, by a preponderance of the evidence, that the publisher acted in a grossly irresponsible manner without due consideration for the standards of information gathering and dissemination ordinarily followed by responsible parties.

Turning to the instant case we look first to the nature of the offending communication. The article at issue here concerned the arrest of a public school teacher for unlawful possession of a hypodermic needle and felony possession of heroin. Thus stated it becomes abundantly clear that the challenged communication falls within the sphere of legitimate public concern. Chapadeau's occupation, one highly influential with the youth of the community, coupled with the oft-cited menace of heroin addiction makes further expatiation unnecessary. The question then becomes whether the appellant submitted evidence sufficient to raise an issue of fact as to the newspaper's culpability.

Appellant asserts that respondent printed the article although it had no source indicating that Chapadeau was in Brookwood Park on that day or that he was arrested at a party there. Neither the Herkimer police captain who had been interviewed, nor the police record which had been examined, indicated that Chapadeau was associated with the other two persons arrested. Additionally, appellant contends that the failure of the State desk reporter and the copy reader to catch the error should preclude summary judgment. We disagree. These factors alone are insufficient to raise a question as to grossly irresponsible conduct. On the contrary they prove the opposite. The instant article was written only after two authoritative sources had been consulted and it was not published until it had been checked by at least two persons other than the writer. This is hardly indicative of gross irresponsibility. Rather it appears that the publisher exercised reasonable methods to insure accuracy.

The mere fact that the word trio was mistakenly substituted for the word duo should not, of itself, result in liability. A limited number of typographical errors, as this appears to be, are inevitable.

Accordingly, the order of the Appellate Division should be affirmed.

## GOODRICH v. WATERBURY REPUBLICAN–AMERICAN, INC.

448 A.2d 1317 (Conn. 1982)

Daly, Associate Justice.

The plaintiff brought this action to recover damages for allegedly libelous statements that were printed about him in the defendant newspaper in November 1974. When all the evidence was in, the court directed a verdict for the defendant. The plaintiff appeals from the final judgment and assigns as error the court's action in directing the verdict and in refusing to set the verdict aside. "In reviewing the action of the trial court, in first directing and thereafter refusing to set aside the verdict, we consider the evidence, including inferences which reasonably may be drawn from this evidence, in the light most favorable to the plaintiff." * * *

[The record below indicated the following relevant facts: the plaintiff was a real estate builder and developer in Middlebury, Connecticut. He also owned a shopping center in Middlebury Hamlet. In getting a permit to develop the shopping center, the plaintiff agreed to fulfill three conditions to ready the land properly required by the planning commission. Despite the promises, the planning commission became concerned about drainage issues. The plaintiff told the commission that he had addressed the problems. As a result, the commission approved new deadlines for compliance. By the time of its next meeting in November, the plaintiff was in default on his construction mortgage, which was subsequently foreclosed.

[The defendant's reporter attended the November meeting of the commission. She wrote articles in the paper that contained statements that the plaintiff requested the newspaper to retract. The defendant refused to do so, leading to the plaintiff's suit. His suit claimed that the stories about him were libelous and invaded his privacy. The defendant raised two defenses: truth and the privilege of "fair comment."] * * *

IA

In a civil action for libel, where the protected interest is personal reputation, the rule in Connecticut is that the truth of an allegedly libelous statement of fact provides an absolute defense. * * * Contrary to the common law rule that required the defendant to establish the literal truth of the precise statement made, the modern rule is that only substantial proof need be shown to constitute the justification. * * * It is not necessary for the defendant to prove the truth of every word of the libel. If he succeeds in proving that "the main charge, or gist, of the libel is true, he need not justify statements or comments which do not add to the sting of the charge or introduce any matter by itself actionable." * * * The issue is whether the libel, as published, would have a different effect on the reader than the pleaded truth would have produced. * * *

Upon examining the statements complained about by the plaintiff, we note that three of them are clearly factual. * * * We need not inquire further, however, since the plaintiff conceded during direct examination that these statements were true, and this concession creates an absolute bar to his claim of libel as to these statements. * * *

The remaining allegations of libel consist of statements of fact combined with opinions or comments based upon those facts. Although some authorities have applied the defense of truth in such circumstances; * * * others have expressly limited the defense of truth to justify only statements of fact. * * * We need not choose between these authorities, however, for "[w]here the comment or opinion deals with matters of public interest, the privilege of 'fair comment' is involved which affords immunity of considerably wider latitude." * * *

B

The privilege of "fair comment," which was one of the most important privileges realized at common law, was a qualified privilege to express an opinion or otherwise comment on matters of public interest. * * * "Traditionally, fair comment concerned persons, institutions or groups who voluntarily injected themselves into the public scene or affected the community's welfare, such as public officials, political candidates, community leaders from the private sector of *private enterprises which affected public welfare*...." * * * The privilege was elevated to constitutional status, however, by a number of United States Supreme Court cases * * *.

In *New York Times Co.*, the court * * * rejected the common law standard of malice and held that media defendants were not liable for defamatory statements of fact or opinion about a public official absent proof that a statement was published with " '*actual* malice'—that is, with knowledge that it was false or not." * * * The constitutional privilege was first extended to public figures; * * * and later to private individuals who became involuntarily associated with matters of "public or general concern." * * * In both of those cases, the plaintiff was still required to prove the "actual malice" standard of *New York Times Co.*

[Later the Supreme Court reconsidered the rule regarding private individuals who became involuntarily associated with matters of public concern.] * * * [It] reestablished the *New York Times* approach of varying the level of constitutional privilege for defamatory falsehood according to the *status* of the person defamed. * * * The court held that "so long as they do not impose liability without fault, the states may define for themselves the appropriate standard of liability for a publisher or broadcaster of a defamatory falsehood injurious to a private individual." * * * [The court then noted that this standard applies only to factual statements and that "the mere comment or opinion on public matters, even though defamatory, enjoys the *unqualified* protection of the First Amendment..."]

As a general rule, therefore, an opinion is privileged as fair comment "only when the facts on which it is based are truly *stated* or *privileged* or otherwise *known* either because the facts are of common knowledge or because, though perhaps unknown to a particular recipient of the communication, they are readily accessible to him." * * *. If the facts that are criticized or commented upon are *not* stated or known, however, then fair comment is no defense. The reason for this distinction is as follows: an opinion must be based upon facts; if the facts are neither known nor stated, then a defamatory opinion implies that there are undisclosed defamatory facts which justify the opinion. * * * The damage of such an implication is that the person defamed becomes the victim of the prejudiced and distorted judgment of not only the defamer, but also of everyone who hears and believes the opinion without knowing that it is based on incorrect and untrue facts. The precise contours of the privilege of fair comment have never been fully articulated, since the United States Supreme Court chose to lay down broad rules of general application rather than opt for an ad hoc resolution of the competing interests in each case. * * * Our review of the case law from *New York Times Co.* through *Gertz*, however, leads us to conclude that expressions of "pure" opinion (those based upon known or disclosed facts) are guaranteed virtually complete constitutional protection. Expressions of "mixed" opinion, however, are privileged only where made (1) by members of the press or news media; (2) about matters of public interest or concern; and (3) without knowingly or recklessly distorting the facts upon which they are based. * * *

[The court then noted that whether the articles are privileged as fair comment is an issue of law. It then found that the news articles in the case before the court were a matter of public interest because the plaintiff was clearly engaged in a private enterprise that affected the public welfare. But it then observed that whether the defendant abused the privilege was a matter of fact and that, given the lower court's grant of the defendant's motion for a directed verdict, the court had to view the evidence in a light most favorable to the plaintiff.]

As in the defense of truth, the privilege of fair comment requires us to read the allegedly libelous articles in their totality, in the context in which they were published. * * * "In order for a statement to be defended as fair comment it must be recognizable by the ordinary reasonable person as opinion and not as a statement of fact." * * * In applying this test, however, "[t]he court must consider all the words used, not merely a particular phrase or sentence. In addition, the court must give weight to cautionary terms used by the person publishing the statement. Finally, the court must consider all of the circumstances surrounding the statement, including the medium by which the statement is disseminated and the audience to which it is published." * * *

C

* * * Accordingly, we conclude that the defendant was performing its wholly legitimate function as a newspaper in publishing articles arising from a public hearing involving a local real estate developer and builder. * * *

Since a reasonable person could only view those comments as pure expressions of opinion, which are unqualifiedly protected by the first amendment * * *, the court properly directed a verdict.

II

In his complaint, the plaintiff also raised one count for invasion of privacy, alleging that the defendant's publication of his financial affairs placed him in a false light before the public. The defendant claimed by way of special defense that the publications were of public interest and newsworthy and that they did not violate the plaintiff's privacy.

The right of privacy, which this court has not previously recognized, has been defined as "the right to be let alone." * * * The origins of this right, which was not expressly recognized at common law, can be directly traced to an 1890 article written by Samuel Warren and Louis Brandeis entitled "The Right to Privacy." Although the early cases were divided, the right became widely accepted after it was recognized by the American Law Institute in 1938. * * * In reviewing the body of privacy law today, we note that tort actions for invasion of privacy have been judicially recognized, in one form or another, in approximately three quarters of the states. * * * On the other hand, the courts which have refused to recognize this right of action have concluded that this issue was more properly one for legislative determination. * * * We do not agree.

There is substantive support today for the conclusion that privacy is a basic right entitled to legal protection. * * * In recognizing this cause of action for invasion of privacy in Connecticut, we quote with approval the language used by the Supreme Court of Oklahoma when it recently recognized the right of privacy: "Although there was no distinctive tort of invasion of privacy in early common law, it has evolved in most jurisdictions based on common law principles sometimes compared to trespass. It is unnecessary for the Legislature to enact a law to create this tort in abrogation of the common law. The common law ... refers not only to the ancient unwritten law of England, but also to that body of law created and preserved by decisions of courts. The common law is not static, but is a dynamic and growing thing and its rules arise from the application of reason to the changing conditions of society." * * * Indeed, as the United States Supreme Court noted * * * "[t]his flexibility and capacity for growth and adaptation is the peculiar boast and excellence of the common law," and this reasoning has been followed by a number of courts that have recognized the privacy right of action. * * *

In recognizing this right of action today, we note that the law of privacy has not developed as a single tort, but as a complex of "four distinct kinds of invasion of four different interests of the plaintiff, which are tied together by the common name, but otherwise have almost nothing in common except that each represents an interference with the right of the plaintiff 'to be let alone.'" * * * The four categories of invasion of privacy are set forth in 3 Restatement (Second), Torts § 652A as follows: (a) unreasonable intrusion upon the seclusion of another; (b) appropriation of the other's name or likeness; (c) unreasonable publicity given to the other's private life; or (d) publicity that unreasonably places the other in a false light before the public. * * *

Count three of the plaintiff's complaint raises a claim for publicity which unreasonably placed him in a false light before the public. To the extent that freedom of the press is involved in this claim, federal law is relevant. * * * The United States Supreme Court first considered the parameters of false light invasions of privacy in *Time, Inc. v. Hill*, 385 U.S. 374, 87 S.Ct. 534, 17 L.Ed.2d 456 (1967). In construing New York's statutory right of privacy against the requirements of the first amendment, the court held that the "actual malice" standard of *New York Times v. Sullivan* was applicable to privacy actions. "We hold that the constitutional protections for speech and press preclude the application of the ... statute to redress false reports of matters of *public interest* in the absence of proof that the defendant published the report with knowledge of its falsity or in reckless disregard of the truth." * * * Thus, matters of public interest were considered newsworthy and a media defendant could not be found liable for a false light invasion of privacy of a private person resulting from erroneous statements that were innocently or even negligently made. * * * The court noted, however, that "[t]his limitation to *newsworthy* persons and events does not of course foreclose an interpretation ... to allow damages where '[r]evelations may be so intimate and so unwarranted in view of the victim's position as to outrage the community's notions of decency.'" * * *

A number of state and federal courts have applied the Restatement rule that a false light invasion of privacy occurs if "(a) the false light in which the other was placed would be highly offensive to a reasonable person, and (b) the actor had knowledge of or acted in reckless disregard as to the falsity of the publicized matter and the false light in which the other would be placed." * * * This form of invasion of privacy protects one's interest in not being placed before the public in an objectionable false light or false position, "or in other words, otherwise than as he is..." * * * The essence of a false light privacy claim is that the matter published concerning the plaintiff (1) is not true; * * * and (2) is such a "major misrepresentation of his character, history, activities or beliefs that serious offense may reasonably be expected to be taken by a reasonable man in his position." * * *

Applying these standards to the present case, we note that the plaintiff conceded during direct examination that the published statements concerning his financial affairs were true, and this defeats his claim for a false light invasion of privacy. Nor can he recover for the claim made in count three of the complaint that "[d]espite the truth of such statements there exist additional circumstances which when expanded, cast the plaintiff in *a more favorable light* more in keeping with reality." * * * To allow recovery upon such a claim would violate the defendant's first amendment rights, since "[t]he choice of material to go into a newspaper, and the decisions made as to limitations on the size and content of the paper, and treatment of public issues and public officials—whether fair or unfair—constitute the exercise of editorial control and judgment." * * * Under the first amendment, a media defendant can be liable for a false light invasion of privacy only where it publishes highly offensive material without regard to its falsity, and to the false impression relayed to the public. * * * As long as the matter published is substantially true, the defendant was constitutionally protected from liability for a false light invasion of privacy, regardless of its decision to omit facts that may place the plaintiff under less harsh public scrutiny.

Finally, although the complaint appears to allege only a false light invasion of privacy claim, to the extent that the publications involved matters of public interest, this claim overlaps that for unreasonable publicity given to one's private life. * * * This claim is also governed by first amendment principles. * * * Such a "private facts" claim is actionable only if the matter publicized is of a kind that "(a) would be highly offensive to a reasonable person, and (b) is not of *legitimate concern* to the public." * * * A media defendant is constitutionally permitted to publicize facts concerning an individual's private life so long as those facts are newsworthy; * * * and in conducting this inquiry we consider "[1] the social value of the facts published, [2] the depth of the article's intrusion into ostensibly private affairs, and [3] the extent to which the party voluntarily acceded to a position of public notoriety." * * *

Applying these principles here, we note that the construction of the Hamlet was clearly a matter of legitimate interest to the community. The articles published financial facts that were relevant to the completion of the mall, and did not intrude into his otherwise private affairs. Lastly, the plaintiff voluntarily injected himself into the public eye by engaging in an enterprise which affected the public welfare. Indeed, "[i]t is not necessary that persons actively seek publicity in order to be found in the 'public eye.' " * * * Accordingly, the right of privacy must give way when balanced against the publication of matters of public interest, in order to insure the "uninhibited, robust and wide-open" discussion of legitimate public issues. * * *

We hold that the right to publicize newsworthy matters would, as a matter of law, extend to the general subject of these articles and that reasonable minds could not differ that the specific financial facts published were also newsworthy. * * * Furthermore, the articles here merely published information about the plaintiff's finances that were already matters of public record, such as liens and lawsuits filed against him, and this fact defeats the claim that his privacy was invaded by their publication. * * * Accordingly, the trial court did not err in directing a verdict as to this count.

## KNIZE v. KNIZE

998 A.2d 198 (Conn. App. 2010)

PER CURIAM.

The pro se plaintiff, Francis Knize, brought an action against the defendant, Waverly Knize, his former wife, for "[l]ibel, [s]lander and [c]haracter [d]efamation," as more particularly alleged in his amended complaint, claiming monetary damages as a result. The case was tried to the jury, which returned a verdict in favor of the defendant, from which the plaintiff has appealed. On appeal, the plaintiff claims that the court improperly denied his motion to set aside the verdict and for a new trial. We affirm the judgment of the trial court.

After many motions, including the defendant's motion to dismiss, which was denied, and the plaintiff's motions to amend his complaint, the case culminated in a jury verdict on April 17, 2009, in favor of the defendant. The plaintiff filed a motion to set aside the verdict and for a new trial on April 23, 2009, claiming that the verdict was contrary to law and that the evidence furnished no reasonable basis for the jury's conclusion. After oral arguments on May 7, 2009, the court filed a memorandum of decision on May 8, 2009, denying the motion. The court found that the verdict was "not against the evidence," was "not contrary to the law" and that the jury "could reasonably have reached the verdict it did."

Our standard of review of a trial court's denial of a motion to set aside a jury verdict is well settled. * * * A trial court possesses inherent power to set aside a jury verdict if the verdict is against the law or the evidence. * * * It "should not set aside a verdict where it is apparent that there was some evidence upon which the jury might reasonably reach [its] conclusion...." * * * The decision to set aside a verdict "entails the exercise of a broad legal discretion ... that, in the absence of clear abuse, we shall not disturb.") * * *

The plaintiff, in his brief, argues that the court applied an improper standard of proof. Specifically, he contends that the standard of proof to be used by the jury should have been clear and convincing evidence for it to find criminal drug abuse by the plaintiff. The issue before the jury, however, was not whether the plaintiff was guilty of crimes related to the use of drugs, but whether the defendant had made libelous statements about the plaintiff concerning his drug abuse, as alleged in his complaint. The plaintiff does not argue in his brief that the standard of proof required for the jury verdict in his libel case was erroneous, inadequate or violative of law. The arguments in his brief, citing law from other state jurisdictions, relate to civil cases involving proof of criminal acts, unlike this case. The standard of proof used in those cases is irrelevant in deciding this case.

The plaintiff's argument that the jury had insufficient evidence "reasonably to find criminal drug use" and the standard of proof to find that fact, as previously noted, is irrelevant. The issue in this case was not whether the plaintiff had violated criminal statutes related to drug use but whether the jury by a preponderance of the evidence could find as a preliminary matter, that the defendant had made defamatory statements as alleged in the plaintiff's complaint.[2] The plaintiff's brief does not address any issue related to the latter claim. We will set aside a trial court's ruling on a motion to set aside a verdict only when an abuse of discretion is manifest or an injustice appears to have been done, neither of which is present in this case. We, therefore, affirm the judgment of the court that denied the plaintiff's motion to set aside the verdict and for a new trial.

Conclusion: The judgment is affirmed.

2. The plaintiff, as a private individual, needed to prove by a preponderance of the evidence that the defendant negligently made defamatory statements about him. * * * He did not need to prove his allegations by the higher burden of proof, namely, clear and convincing evidence, which would be true if he were a public official. Id. The plaintiff's argument as to the use of a higher standard of proof for establishing that the plaintiff violated criminal statutes as to drug use might be understood as his belief that the defendant had to prove, as her defense, that the statements about him that he attributed to her were not libelous or defamatory if she could prove by clear and convincing evidence that he had violated criminal statutes related to drug use. It is not for this court, however, to speculate as to why the plaintiff chooses to argue for a higher standard of proof in his case.

# CHAPTER TWO

# PERSONAL JURISDICTION

## I. INTRODUCTION

After consultation with counsel, Ms. Nobile decided to bring an action against Mike Ridge with the hope that the court will enjoin him from publishing a story that will humiliate her and that may destroy her career. She has decided to join as a co-defendant Ridge's employer, MDC, Inc. This chapter includes a number of legal documents that counsel filed on her behalf. After the first set of documents, you will find some questions about how Ms. Nobile should serve process on the defendants. Consider those questions before reading on. Thereafter, you will find additional documents and questions about the defendants' strategic choices.

Your professor may assign the questions in this chapter for discussion in class. For the main part of this simulation, your professor will assign you to represent either Ms. Nobile or Mr. Ridge and MDC, Inc. That will involve defendants' efforts to have this suit dismissed for lack of personal jurisdiction. Your professor may have you argue the question before a magistrate judge or submit a short memorandum in support of your position. As you will see when you read the allegations in the various documents and the evidence elicited in the depositions of two witnesses, this case requires you to explore how a court should resolve a question of personal jurisdiction when the defendants' contacts come about, in part, through activities on the Internet.

Plaintiff's complaint poses an interesting strategic problem. She wants to enjoin publication of Defendant Ridge's story that will claim that the Plaintiff downloaded child pornography onto her office computer. But most court papers, including pleading papers like her complaint, are a matter of public record. In some states, the law states that filings with the court "shall be deemed public records." Courts are hesitant to deny public access to court documents; public policy favors judicial accountability. For the public to have confidence in the court system, members of the public should have access to the information supporting judges' decisions.

Similar problems arise when litigants may be forced to reveal documents containing employees' confidential information like social security numbers or otherwise confidential job assessments, documents containing intellectual property or trade secrets or a host of other kinds of documents containing other private or embarrassing information. The problem existed before the public had access to documents on the Web. The problem is more acute today because many jurisdictions require electronic filing and members of the public have access to those documents on the Web.

Not surprisingly, courts have a remedy to avoid the kind of problem posed by Nobile v. Ridge et al. Litigants can file a motion asking that documents be kept under seal. Litigants must overcome the presumption favoring public access. Local federal district court rules typically contain a provision setting forth procedures governing requests for submitting documents under seal. The party seeking to file a document under seal must seek court approval when the litigant submits the document. The party must include an application and proposed order along with the document. For purposes of this chapter, assume that Ms. Nobile has included such a request and that the court will grant that request.

## II. THE LAWSUIT: THE SUMMONS AND COMPLAINT

This section consists of several legal documents that Ms. Nobile has filed in the United States District Court for the Central District of New York. Initially, she has sought a temporary retraining order, which the court granted. Thereafter, she filed a complaint for an injunction and for damages. After the documents, you will also find some questions about methods of serving the documents on the defendants.

In the United States District Court

for the

Central District of New York

Sarah D. Nobile, )<br>
Plaintiff ) Civil Action No. 00–123<br>
v. )<br>
Michael Ridge and )<br>
MDC, Inc. )<br>
Defendants )

### PLAINTIFF'S MOTION FOR A TEMPORARY RESTRAINING ORDER

Plaintiff Sarah D. Nobile through undersigned counsel hereby applies *ex parte* for a temporary restraining order pursuant to Rule 65 of the Federal Rules of Civil Procedure. Through this motion Plaintiff seeks a temporary restraining order prohibiting Defendant Michael Ridge, his agents, servants, employees, and attorneys and all persons acting in concert with him including his employer, Defendant MDC, Inc., from publishing in any medium, disseminating, or in any manner revealing or disclosing information concerning Plaintiff's alleged involvement with child pornography. Absent the requested temporary restraining order, Defendants intend to publish a story falsely alleging that Plaintiff possessed child pornography on her office computer.

This Court has jurisdiction over this matter based on diversity. Plaintiff is a citizen of New York; Defendant Ridge is a citizen of Connecticut, and Defendant MDC, Inc. is incorporated in Delaware and has its principal place of business in Connecticut.

This motion is based on the following facts: Defendants unlawfully obtained information concerning the results of June 1, YR-03 search of then-Connecticut State Appellate Court Judge John Elliot's chambers. Defendant Ridge has conspired with an unknown individual or individuals to obtain information in a sealed search warrant illegally issued and executed by the Doddville Police Department. If Defendants are not immediately restrained from publishing this information, which is false and defamatory, Plaintiff will experience grave and irreparable harm.

This motion is based on the Memorandum of Points and Authorities attached hereto,[1] the Summons and Complaint on file in this Court.

Respectfully submitted,

*Adrian Connell*

Adrian Connell
139 McGeorge Avenue
Cuomo City, New York 11774
(561) 782–1897

Date: August 6, YR-00

1. A party seeking a TRO would include the Memorandum of Points and Authorities. I have not included one. Your professor may assign members of your class the job of drafting such a memorandum.

In the United States District Court

for the

Central District of New York

| | | |
|---|---|---|
| Sarah D. Nobile, | ) | |
| Plaintiff | ) | Civil Action No. 00–123 |
| v. | ) | |
| Michael Ridge and | ) | |
| MDC, Inc. | ) | |
| Defendants | ) | |

**PLAINTIFF SARAH D. NOBILE'S DECLARATION IN SUPPORT OF HER MOTION FOR A TEMPORARY RESTRAINING ORDER**

1. I, Sarah D. Nobile, am the plaintiff in this action against Michael Ridge and MDC, Inc. Defendant Ridge is threatening to publish a false and defamatory story in which he claims falsely that I illegally possessed child pornography on my office computer when I worked for Connecticut State Appellate Judge John Elliot.

2. Neither I nor my attorney has given notice to the Defendants on fear that they will publish the story and, thereby, cause the harm that I hope to prevent.

3. I have read the allegations in **PLAINTIFF'S MOTION FOR A TEMPORARY RESTRAINING ORDER**, and I declare under penalty of perjury that the foregoing information is true and correct.

Executed this day, August 6, YR-00

*Sarah D. Nobile*

Sarah D. Nobile

Respectfully submitted,
*Adrian Connell*

Adrian Connell
139 McGeorge Avenue
Cuomo City, New York 11774
(561) 782–1897

Date: August 6, YR-00

In the United States District Court

for the

Central District of New York

| | | |
|---|---|---|
| Sarah D. Nobile, | ) | |
| Plaintiff | ) | Civil Action No. 00–123 |
| v. | ) | |
| Michael Ridge and | ) | |
| MDC, Inc. | ) | |
| Defendants | ) | |

## TEMPORARY RESTRAINING ORDER AND ORDER TO SHOW CAUSE

This court heard this cause on August 7, YR-00, on Plaintiff's Motion for a Temporary Restraining Order. This court considered not only her motion, but also the Plaintiff's Declaration in Support of her motion. In light of her allegations of harm that would result from giving Defendants notice of the hearing before the court, this court agreed to proceed *ex parte*. This court makes the following findings of fact, conclusions of law, and enters the following order.

### Findings of Fact

In June, YR-03, Doddville Police executed a search warrant at Plaintiff's place of work, the chambers of Connecticut State Appellate Court Judge John Elliot. Police seized two computers from chambers and later found files containing child pornography. Lacking evidence sufficient to demonstrate that Plaintiff downloaded the files, the Doddville District Attorney's Office refused to prosecute the case. Because of the sensitive nature of the information in the search warrant, the affidavit, and return on the warrant, the District Attorney agreed to seal the documents.

In August of this year, Plaintiff learned that Defendant Michael Ridge planned to publish information learned from those sealed documents. Without opportunity for discovery, Plaintiff has not had a chance to demonstrate that the Defendant's acquisition of that information was illegal. But given the nature of the documents, this court has drawn the inference that Defendant has gained access through some illegal conduct. Plaintiff alleges that she never possessed child pornography and any claim to the contrary is false, defamatory and harmful. Without an opportunity for an evidentiary hearing, this court accepts as true those allegations.

This court finds that, if not restrained, Defendants will publish information that is false and defamatory about Plaintiff and, if the story is not defamatory, it will portray Plaintiff in a false light. Plaintiff will suffer irreparable harm if Defendants publish the story.

## CONCLUSIONS OF LAW

Plaintiff has demonstrated a probability of success on the merits of her claim, alternatively, for defamation or for an invasion of privacy.

At this point in the proceedings, this court does not find any plausible defense that would prevent a temporary order to preserve the status quo.

## TEMPORARY RESTRAINING ORDER

Defendants Michael Ridge and MDC, Inc., their agents, servants, employees, attorneys, and all persons acting in concert with them are temporarily restrained and enjoined from publishing in any medium, including but not limited to books, newspapers, magazines, radio, television or any site on the Internet or World Wide Web, disseminating or in any other manner disclosing information learned from the sealed documents implicating Plaintiff in criminal activity.

This Temporary Restraining Order shall remain in effect for ten days, unless Plaintiff fails to pay security in the sum of Twenty Thousand Dollars ($20,000) for payment of such costs and damages that may be suffered by any party who may be wrongfully enjoined.

## ORDER TO SHOW CAUSE

Defendants Michael Ridge and MDC, Inc. are hereby ordered to appear before this court to show cause why a preliminary injunction to the same effect as the Temporary Restraining Order should not be granted and kept in effect until a full trial on the merits. The show cause hearing shall be held on August 14, YR-00, at 9:00 a.m. in Courtroom A in the United States District Court for the Central District of New York.

Dated: August 7, YR-00.
*John Jay Leach*

John Jay Leach
United States District Judge

In the United States District Court

for the

Central District of New York

| | | |
|---|---|---|
| Sarah D. Nobile,<br>Plaintiff<br>v.<br>Michael Ridge and<br>MDC, Inc.<br>Defendants | )<br>)<br>)<br>)<br>)<br>) | Civil Action No. 00–123 |

## COMPLAINT FOR INJUNCTIVE RELIEF AND FOR DAMAGES FOR DEFAMATION AND INVASION OF PRIVACY

Plaintiff Sarah D. Nobile, on personal knowledge as to its own acts, and on information and belief as to all others based on its investigation, alleges as follows:

### INTRODUCTION

1. Plaintiff, Sarah D. Nobile, brings this action to prevent Defendant, Michael Ridge, from publishing a story that the Defendant knows to be false and misleading, putting the Plaintiff in a false light and that will damage her irreparably. She joins as co-Defendant MDC, Inc., Defendant Ridge's employer.

### STATEMENT OF JURISDICTION

2. Plaintiff, Sarah D. Nobile, is a citizen of the State of New York. Defendant Michael Ridge is a citizen of the State of Connecticut. Defendant MDC, Inc. is a citizen of Delaware, its state of incorporation, and Connecticut, its principal place of business.

3. The amount in controversy, without interest and costs, exceeds the sum or value specified in 28 U.S.C. § 1332.

### FACTUAL BACKGROUND

4. On August 28, YR-05, Plaintiff began working for Connecticut State Judge John Elliot.

5. During her period of employment for Judge Elliot, Plaintiff worked in Judge Elliot's Chambers in the Appellate Court Building, 123 Nutley Avenue, Harford, Connecticut.

6. As part of her job, Plaintiff was assigned a workstation in an office shared with Judge Elliot's other law clerk, Nathan Loewe.

7. Plaintiff's workstation included a Dell Computer, with access to the Internet, which she was allowed to use to conduct legal research on various legal data bases.

8. At all times, Plaintiff followed office policy and used her computer for proper business purposes only.

9. On June 1, YR-03, members of Doddville City Police Department [Police Department, hereinafter] executed a search warrant for Judge Elliot's chambers.

10. During the course of the search, a member of the Police Department removed two computers from Judge Elliot's chambers.

11. On June 10, YR-03, a technician working for the Police Department, allegedly found child pornography on two of the computers, including the Plaintiff's.

12. Because of serious questions about the legality of the warrant and because many other people had access to the computers, the Doddville District Attorney's Office refused to prosecute Plaintiff.

13. For reasons stated in Paragraph 12, the Doddville District Attorney Clara Saint-Jean agreed to seal the warrant because of concerns that revealing information about the search would unfairly damage Plaintiff's and others' reputations.

14. On August 3, YR-00, Plaintiff received a phone call from Judge Elliot's former secretary, Rhoda Sheen, who told her that Defendant Michael Ridge was threatening to publish an article claiming that Plaintiff and Judge Elliot were guilty of possessing child pornography on their office computers.

15. Also on August 3, YR-00, with the hope of stopping the publication of a false and defamatory story, Plaintiff called Defendant Ridge and left a voicemail in which she told him of her concerns.

16. Defendant Ridge called Plaintiff on August 4, YR-00 and told her that he was going to name her in the story and post it on his blog, GOTCHA! He also told her that the main focus of the story was Judge Elliot, whom Defendant Ridge called a hypocrite, and intimated that if Plaintiff would be a source confirming the facts in the story about the Judge, he would delete her name.

17. Plaintiff begged for time to consider what to do. She brings this suit to stop publication of a false and defamatory article that may go "viral" on the Internet, permanently harming her reputation.

### COUNT ONE

18. Paragraphs 4-17 are hereby incorporated by reference. Defendant Ridge's story alleging that Plaintiff possessed child pornography is false and defamatory.

### COUNT TWO

19. Paragraphs 4-17 are hereby incorporated by reference. Defendant Ridge's story alleging that Plaintiff possessed child pornography violates her right to privacy. Specifically, even a statement limited to the fact that child pornography was found on her computer puts Plaintiff in a false light.

## COUNT THREE

20. Paragraphs 4-17 are hereby incorporated by reference. Defendant MDC, Inc. is liable to Plaintiff under the theory of respondeat superior as Defendant Ridge's employer.

## PRAYER FOR RELIEF

21. Plaintiff requests that this Court temporarily during the pendency of this action restrain Defendant Ridge and all persons acting in concert with Defendant Ridge from publishing or otherwise disseminating any story concerning Plaintiff that alleges that child pornography was found on her computer or in any other way linking her to illegal activity based on the search of Judge Elliot's chambers.

22. Plaintiff requests that this Court enjoin Defendant Ridge and all persons acting in concert with Defendant Ridge from publishing or otherwise disseminating any story concerning Plaintiff that alleges that child pornography was found on her computer or in any other way linking her to illegal activity based on the search of Judge Elliot's chambers.

23. Plaintiff requests that this Court temporarily during the pendency of this action and permanently enjoin Defendant Ridge from publishing or disseminating in any manner a copy of the search warrant issued for the search of Judge Elliot's office dated May 26, YR-03 or any information learned from examination of that document.

24. Plaintiff requests that this Court temporarily during the pendency of this action and permanently enjoin Defendant Ridge from publishing or disseminating in any manner a copy of any other documents relating to the search warrant issued for the search of Judge Elliot's office dated May 26, YR-03 or any information learned from examination of those documents, including but not limited to the Affidavit of Probable Cause and the Return on the Warrant.

25. Plaintiff requests compensatory damages in such amount as the court shall determine to compensate Plaintiff for her damages suffered as a result of Defendant Ridge's conduct. She requests that the Court enter judgment for those damages against Defendant Ridge and/or Defendant MDC, Inc.

26. Plaintiff requests punitive damages in such amount as the court shall determine to punish Defendant Ridge for his outrageous and unlawful conduct. She requests that the Court enter judgment for those damages against Defendant Ridge and/or Defendant MDC, Inc.

29. Plaintiff requests her costs of suit and reasonable attorneys' fees;

30. Plaintiff requests such other relief to which she may be entitled.

Respectfully submitted,

*Adrian Connell*
Adrian Connell
139 McGeorge Avenue
Cuomo City, New York 11774
(561) 782–1897

Dated: August 6, YR-00

In the United States District Court

for the

Central District of New York

| | | |
|---|---|---|
| Sarah D. Nobile,<br>Plaintiff<br>v.<br>Michael Ridge and<br>MDC, Inc.<br>Defendants | )<br>)<br>)<br>)<br>)<br>) | Civil Action No. 00–123 |

SUMMONS

Within 21 days after service of this summons on you (not counting the day you received it), you must serve on the plaintiff an answer to the attached complaint or a motion under Rule 12 of the Federal Rules of Civil Procedure. The answer or motion must be served on the plaintiff's attorney, Adrian Connell, whose address is 139 McGeorge Avenue, Cuomo City, New York 11774. If you fail to do so, judgment by default will be entered against you for the relief demanded in the complaint. You also must file your answer or motion with the court.

Date: August 9, YR-00 *Jeremy Brighton*

Clerk of Court[2]

Before reading further, consider the following questions:

One concern that counsel for the plaintiff must decide is how to serve the defendants with the various legal documents. Because the plaintiff has chosen to file in federal court, federal procedural rules apply. At this point, how do the Federal Rules of Civil Procedure contemplate that a plaintiff will serve the defendant with process? What is the most reliable way to serve process? Why would the plaintiff chose a form of service other than the best method for assuring that the defendants will receive actual notice? Examine Rule 4 of the F.R.C.P. The three sub-rules of relevance to Nobile v. Ridge are Rules 4(e), (h) and (k). What are the various methods available to the plaintiff?

---

**2.** Counsel for Plaintiff prepared a separate summons for Defendant MDC, Inc., and served that along with the complaint and the order granting the Temporary Restraining Order.

# III. ASSURING ADEQUATE NOTICE: SERVING PROCESS

In the United States District Court

for the

Central District of New York

| | | |
|---|---|---|
| Sarah D. Nobile, | ) | |
| Plaintiff | ) | Civil Action No. 00–123 |
| v. | ) | Declaration of Service |
| Michael Ridge and | ) | Person Served: Michael Ridge |
| MDC, Inc. | ) | Date Served: August 10, YR-00 |
| Defendants | ) | |

I, the undersigned declare under penalty of perjury that I am over the age of eighteen years and not a party to this action; that I served the above named person the following documents:

in the following manner: (check one)

1) By personally delivering copies to the person served. √

2) By leaving, during usual office hours, copies in the office of the person served with the person who apparently was in charge and thereafter mailing (by first-class mail, postage prepaid) copies to the person served at the place where the copies were left.

3) By leaving copies at the dwelling house, usual place of abode, or usual place of business of the person served in the presence of a competent member of the household or a person apparently in charge of his office or place of business, at least 18 years of age, who was informed of the general nature of the papers, and thereafter mailing (by first-class mail, postage prepaid) copies to the person served at the place where the copies were left.

4) By placing a copy in a separate envelope, with postage fully prepaid, for each address named below and depositing each in the U.S. mail at ___ on ___, 20___

Executed on August 10, YR-00 at 11:00 a.m.

*Jeremy Taylor*

In the United States District Court

for the

Central District of New York

| | | |
|---|---|---|
| Sarah D. Nobile, | ) | |
| Plaintiff | ) | Civil Action No. 00–123 |
| v. | ) | Declaration of Service |
| Michael Ridge and | ) | Person Served: Royce Jenkins |
| MDC, Inc. | ) | (agent, MDC, Inc.) |
| Defendants | ) | Date Served: August 10, YR-00 |

I, the undersigned declare under penalty of perjury that I am over the age of eighteen years and not a party to this action; that I served the above named person the following documents:

in the following manner: (check one)

1) By personally delivering copies to the person served. √

2) By leaving, during usual office hours, copies in the office of the person served with the person who apparently was in charge and thereafter mailing (by first-class mail, postage prepaid) copies to the person served at the place where the copies were left.

3) By leaving copies at the dwelling house, usual place of abode, or usual place of business of the person served in the presence of a competent member of the household or a person apparently in charge of his office or place of business, at least 18 years of age, who was informed of the general nature of the papers, and thereafter mailing (by first-class mail, postage prepaid) copies to the person served at the place where the copies were left.

4) By placing a copy in a separate envelope, with postage fully prepaid, for each address named below and depositing each in the U.S. mail at ___ on ___, 20___

Executed on August 10, YR-00 at 11:00 a.m.

*Jeremy Taylor*

## IV. THE DEFENDANTS' RESPONSE

Before reading further, after the plaintiff has served the defendants with process, counsel for the defendants must consider how to respond to the plaintiff's suit. One option would be to do nothing, thereby allowing the plaintiff to ask that a default judgment be entered against the defendants. That has advantages: if the defendants do not have a strong case on the merits, they may prefer to stay home and force the plaintiff to come to their jurisdiction to enforce the judgment. But in a case in which defendants have plausible defenses, they risk losing those defenses: when the plaintiff comes to their jurisdiction with judgment in hand, the plaintiff will file an action to collect on the judgment and ask the court to give full faith and credit to the earlier judgment. The defendants can try to avoid enforcement of the judgment but are limited in the kinds of challenges that they can make; notably, they can contend that the rendering court lacked personal jurisdiction over the defendants. If they fail in that challenge, they cannot now try the cases on the merits.

Thus, for purposes of this assignment, the defendants have decided to appear in the action in New York. Before you read further, consider what their options are at this point by focusing on Rule 12, F.R.C.P. In many state systems, defendants who hope to challenge personal jurisdiction must enter a special appearance. If you examine Rule 12 closely, you will see that the defendants do not make a special appearance to contest jurisdiction. Explore what their options are and consider which route makes the most sense.

## V. THE DEFENDANTS' MOTION

In the United States District Court

for the

Central District of New York

| | | |
|---|---|---|
| Sarah D. Nobile, | ) | |
| Plaintiff | ) | Civil Action No. 00–123 |
| v. | ) | |
| Michael Ridge and | ) | |
| MDC, Inc. | ) | |
| Defendants | ) | |

**DEFENDANT RIDGE'S MOTION TO DISMISS UNDER RULE 12(b) FOR LACK OF PERSONAL JURISDICTION AND IMPROPER VENUE AND FOR FAILURE TO STATE A CLAIM FOR RELIEF**

The defendant moves to dismiss this action because:

1. This Court lacks personal jurisdiction over Defendant Michael Ridge because service was effected under New York law, N.Y. C.P.L.R. § 302. Jurisdiction is improper because Plaintiff's action is for defamation and, as such, does not come within the requirements of New York law.[3]

---

3. The relevant sections of § 302 follow:

**Personal jurisdiction by acts of non-domiciliaries**

(a) Acts which are the basis of jurisdiction. As to a cause of action arising from any of the acts enumerated in this section, a court may exercise personal jurisdiction over any non-domiciliary, or his executor or administrator, who in person or through an agent:

1. transacts any business within the state or contracts anywhere to supply goods or services in the state; or

2. This Court lacks personal jurisdiction over Defendant Michael Ridge because the assertion of jurisdiction violates the Due Process Clause of the Fourteenth Amendment.

3. Venue is improper in this district because the Defendants do not reside in this district and none of the events took place in this district; as a result, the case should be dismissed.

4. This Court should dismiss because Plaintiff's complaint fails to state a claim for relief.

Dated: August 26, YR-00

Respectfully submitted,

*R. Cooper Russell*
R. Cooper Russell
Russell and Scott
Attorneys at Law
Suite 6
McGeorge Towers
Cuomo City, New York 11774
(561) 782–0099
Attorney for Defendant Michael Ridge[4]

---

2. commits a tortious act within the state, except as to a cause of action for defamation of character arising from the act; or
3. commits a tortious act without the state causing injury to person or property within the state, except as to a cause of action for defamation of character arising from the act, if he
(i) regularly does or solicits business, or engages in any other persistent course of conduct, or derives substantial revenue from goods used or consumed or services rendered, in the state, or
(ii) expects or should reasonably expect the act to have consequences in the state and derives substantial revenue from interstate or international commerce; * * *

**4.** The defendant would also attach a Memorandum of Points and Authorities along with the Motion. Your professor may assign students the job of drafting such a memorandum.

In the United States District Court

for the

Central District of New York

Sarah D. Nobile, )
Plaintiff ) Civil Action No. 00–123
v. )
Michael Ridge and )
MDC, Inc. )
Defendants )

**CERTIFICATE OF SERVICE**

I hereby certify that on August 26, YR-00, I caused the following document:

DEFENDANT RIDGE'S MOTION TO DISMISS UNDER RULE 12(b) FOR LACK OF PERSONAL JURISDICTION AND IMPROPER VENUE AND FOR FAILURE TO STATE A CLAIM FOR RELIEF

to be served on the plaintiff and plaintiff's counsel, Adrian Connell, by first-class mail, postage paid.

Dated: August 26, YR-00

Respectfully submitted,

*R. Cooper Russell*
R. Cooper Russell
Russell and Scott
Attorneys at Law
Suite 6
McGeorge Towers
Cuomo City, New York 11774
(561) 782–0099
Attorney for Defendant Michael Ridge

# VI. THE FACTUAL RECORD

The defendant has raised separate grounds upon which to dismiss. At this point, the United States District Court has a number of options. It may resolve each matter separately. That may be the best strategy if one ground for dismissal seems particularly strong. Further, when a defendant challenges the assertion of personal jurisdiction, s/he is arguing, in part, that trying the case in the forum is too burdensome. If that is the case, the court may be concerned that requiring a hearing on all of the grounds for dismissal adds to that burden. As a result, the court may sensibly resolve the personal jurisdiction issue first.

Another question at this stage is how much discovery to allow in connection with a defendant's challenge to personal jurisdiction. As summarized by the District Court in *McNamee v. Clemens,* 762 F. Supp. 2d 584 (E.D.N.Y. 2011):

> On a motion to dismiss, the plaintiff bears the burden of showing that the court has jurisdiction over the defendants. * * * "In order to survive a motion to dismiss for lack of personal jurisdiction, a plaintiff must make a prima facie showing that jurisdiction exists." * * * However, prior to discovery, where a court relies on pleadings and affidavits, a plaintiff may defeat a motion to dismiss by producing "legally sufficient allegations of jurisdiction." * * * The pleadings must be credited as true and doubts are resolved in the plaintiff's favor. * * *

In some cases, the court allows the party to engage in further discovery, including interrogatories and depositions, but limited to facts relating to the assertion of personal jurisdiction. Where a paper record resulting from discovery may not resolve all of the issues, a court may order an evidentiary hearing to resolve matters of credibility.

Not satisfied with Plaintiff's allegations in Nobile v. Ridge, Judge John Jay Leach, before whom the case is pending, referred the matter to Magistrate Judge Carla Bricker. Judge Bricker has granted Ms. Connell's request to conduct two depositions, the first of Michael Ridge and the second, Jocelyn Raider, a vice president of MDC, Inc.[5] Relevant parts of those depositions appear below.

5. Under Rule 30(b)(6) of the Federal Rules of Civil Procedure, when a party wants to take a deposition of a business organization, one option is to describe the matters for examination and then allow the business organization to produce a person with relevant information.

In the United States District Court

for the

Central District of New York

| | | |
|---|---|---|
| Sarah D. Nobile,<br>Plaintiff<br>v.<br>Michael Ridge and<br>MDC, Inc.<br>Defendants | )<br>)<br>)<br>)<br>)<br>) | Civil Action No. 00–123 |

**DEPOSITION OF MICHAEL RIDGE**

Taken by Plaintiff, at Law Offices of Preston Pearson, Attorney at Law, Suite 9, the Frank Building, Dodd Plaza, Doddville, Connecticut, commencing at 9:30 a.m., September 16, YR-00.

Appearances

For Plaintiff:

Adrian Connell
139 McGeorge Avenue
Cuomo City, New York 11774
(561) 782–1897

For Defendants:

R. Cooper Russell
Russell and Scott
Attorneys at Law
Suite 6
McGeorge Towers
Cuomo City, New York 11774
(561) 782–0099

Having been duly sworn, Michael Ridge testified as follows:

MS. CONNELL:

Q. Good morning. For the record, Mr. Ridge, you are represented by Mr. Russell, and you are aware that he also represents MDC, Inc., your co-defendant?

A. I am indeed aware.

Q. And has counsel, Mr. Russell, explained any possible conflict of interests that may arise?

MR. RUSSELL: Objection, Adrian. That touches on my advice to Mr. Ridge. If this will shorten the matter, both parties have agreed to my representation at this point, for purposes of our jurisdictional challenges. In the unlikely case that Judge Leach does not dismiss this action, I am sure we will re-examine the matter. But that, frankly, is not your business.

MS. CONNELL: It may become my business. Changing counsel in mid-stream for purposes of creating delay is a Rule 11 violation.

MR. RUSSELL: We are getting off to the wrong start here. I have other matters to take care of.

MS. CONNELL: You did get us off to a bad start, but I accept your apology. Now, before more asides, Mr. Ridge, would you state your name for the record and spell it for Ms. Watson, our stenographer?

A. I would be glad to. My name is Michael Ridge. Ms. Watson, surely you can spell Michael, a followed by e. And Ridge is R–I–D–G–E, like bridge.

Q. Mr. Ridge, is this your first deposition?

A. No.

Q. How often have you been deposed?

MR. RUSSELL: Objection. How does that relate to the subject of this dispute?

MS. CONNELL: Cooper, I thought that you had other commitments and wanted to make this a smooth process? Judge Bricker does not want to have us before her this afternoon or tomorrow sorting out our differences.

Q. Go ahead and answer, Mr. Ridge.

A. Should I? (directing his question to Mr. Russell).

MR. RUSSELL: Go ahead.

A. Four or five times.

Q. In defamation cases?

A. Yes.

Q. Invasion of privacy?

A. Only once.

Q. You do understand the purpose of the deposition then? The court has entered an order allowing discovery on your motion in Nobile v. Ridge?

A. Yes.

Q. You do understand that you are under oath and that you may be prosecuted for perjury if you do not tell the truth?

A. Sure.

Q. Do you have reservations about telling the truth today?

A. Of course not.

Q. Are you suffering from any impairment today that would not allow you to testify accurately?

A. I am not sure what you mean.

Q. For example, you are not intoxicated or under the influence of any medication?

A. No. I could use some more coffee but no, no drugs or alcohol.

Q. You will have a chance for coffee later, I imagine. How is your overall health today?

A. Good. Very good.

Q. Would you tell me your educational background and qualifications, if any, as a journalist?

A. Sure. I graduated from Connecticut State University's School of Journalism in YR-08. I then went to work for ...

Q. Let me interrupt for a second. I took a look at your Web page. You brag about not having done very well at the University, don't you?

A. I don't brag.

Q. Well, why don't you explain how you did there and why you think that you did not do very well?

A. I would be delighted to do so. I graduated, but I was not one of the chosen. Faculty members at the Journalism School are stuck in the past. They don't understand how the Internet has changed the game. They are stuck in the past, worshipping Murrow and Cronkite.

Q. You mean, they believed in checking sources?

MR. RUSSELL: Adrian, I have to object. Please don't pick a fight with Mr. Ridge.

MS. CONNELL: Mr. Ridge, please continue.

A. Anyway, yes, I had a C average when I graduated.

Q. Did you get a job in journalism when you graduated?

A. I did. My first job was doing stories for a Web site. I wrote copy on medical topics. The offices were located in Hartford.

Q. How long did that last?

A. About six months.

Q. Why did you leave?

A. The work wasn't very challenging.

Q. You were let go, weren't you?

A. I left with a mutual understanding with my employer.

Q. A mutual understanding that you were fired?

A. No, an understanding that I did not like my boss and she didn't like me.

Q. And after you left on those terms, where did you work?

A. I got a job with a Web site that arranged adult dating.

Q. Adult dating?

A. Yeah. Ever try it?

Q. Mr. Ridge, would you explain what adult dating is?

A. Lonely people send in their biographies and try to find someone compatible.

Q. What did that have to do with journalism?

A. I edited their submissions and posted them on the Web site.

Q. How long did that last?

A. About six months. It was not really journalism.

Q. And then?

A. At that time, blogging was really taking off. I realized that I could set up my own Web site, get ads and make a living.

Q. What was the name of your Web site?

A. GOTCHA!

Q. And that is the blog that you still maintain?

A. Yes, except that MDC bought me out and now I work for them.

Q. When did MDC buy you out?

A. About two years ago.

Q. So you are employed by MDC?

A. Yes.

Q. I have seen your blog and your Web page. But I would like you to describe it so that we have that information on the record.

A. Sure. I agree with Mark Twain—you have seen my motto: Politicians are the Criminal Class in America. A lot of bloggers focus on national politicians, but I made my mark by writing about Connecticut politicians mostly. That is why I am so interested in that hypocrite Judge Elliot.

Q. But you don't limit yourself to local politicians, do you?

A. No, occasionally I go with a story from other states. Most of my work is in Hartford or local politicians. Did you see my story about the mayor of Doddville? That was a good one; religious guy using a Doddville credit card to buy time on a porn site.

Q. Tell me about your blog, how many subscribers, for example?

A. Well, we don't have subscribers. Anyone can come to the blog.

Q. How do you and MDC make money?

A. Ads.

Q. Tell me how that works?

A. Depending on the number of hits we get, an advertiser pays us a fee.

Q. How much do you make in a given year?

A. I do okay.

Q. I would like a more specific answer. It is relevant to the court's jurisdiction.

A. I average $40–45 thousand a year. That is from the Web site.

Q. You have other sources of income?

A. Yes.

Q. Like?

A. I sell some of my stories to local news outlets, local magazines.

Q. Where are they distributed?

A. They are almost all in Connecticut.

Q. Are there any in New York?

A. Some.

Q. How many?

A. Four or five.

Q. Okay. So let me go back to your Web site. Do you know where visitors to the site are located?

A. Not really.

Q. Do you sell any products on your website?

A. No.

Q. So you don't get mailing addresses of people who visit your site?

A. That is right.

Q. Do you promote your Web site anywhere outside of Connecticut?

A. Not really.

Q. I am not sure what "not really" means. Does it mean, sometimes? A little bit?

A. Well, I go to conferences now and then and speak about the site.

Q. Where? In New York?

A. New York is not very far from Connecticut. So sure.

Q. Describe the events that you have attended in New York.

A. Well, I went to an event run by Internet News Service at the Hilton in Cuomo City last year.

Q. What was your role?

A. I gave a presentation.

Q. About what?

A. Getting started on the Web.

Q. And what was the content of your presentation?

MR. RUSSELL: Aren't we getting off the subject of this deposition?

MS. CONNELL: Coop, this is highly relevant.

MR. RUSSELL: I fail to see how.

MS. CONNELL: Let him answer and then I will tell you.

Q. Mr. Ridge, do you remember the question?

A. Yes. I spoke about my views about the way the Web is supposed to advance truth.

Q. How is that?

A. Everybody has access to it. So if something is not true, anybody can go on the Web and correct the record.

Q. And so if you defame my client, after her reputation is lost and she loses her job, she can write a rejoinder on your blog?

A. Sure.

Q. You have got to be kidding me.

MR. RUSSELL: Don't badger my client.

MS. CONNELL: I wasn't.

MR. RUSSELL: Come on; let's get this over with.

Q. Mr. Ridge, so most of your stories are about Connecticut politicians, but some are about politicians located in other states, is that right?

A. Yes.

Q. And some of them are in New York, correct?

A. Not very often.

Q. And some of the visitors to your Web site are from New York, correct?

A. I think that I already said yes.

Q. Let's go to the incident that has brought us to this deposition. Who was your source that Ms. Nobile was involved in pornography?

A. Child pornography.

MR. RUSSELL: Don't answer that question.

MS. CONNELL: What is your basis of objection?

MR. RUSSELL: That may be discoverable—I don't concede that point—but if it is discoverable, that will be decided when we get to general discovery. It can have no relevance to the motion we are discussing today.

MS. CONNELL: Of course it can.

MR. RUSSELL: Mr. Ridge, don't answer the question.

MS. CONNELL: R.C., if the source is from New York, that is highly relevant.

MR. RUSSELL: Then ask him one question, "Was your source from New York?" That is it or we go before the judge now.

MS. CONNELL: Was your source from New York or in New York when you got information about Ms. Nobile?

A. Nope.

Q. About a month ago, you called Judge Elliot's retired secretary, didn't you?

A. I did.

Q. And you wanted information about Judge Elliot and about the police raid of his office a little over three years ago, didn't you?

A. I have nothing to hide. You bet I did. The guy portrays himself as a crusader while he is watching kiddy porn on his office computer; that is gross.

Q. And not long after his secretary denied—wait, let me ask another question first. The Judge's secretary also denied that Ms. Nobile had anything to do with child pornography, didn't she?

A. What would you expect her to say?

Q. I will take that as "yes." And you ended up calling Ms. Nobile, didn't you?

A. She called me first.

Q. And you called back after you got her voicemail, didn't you?

A. I did.

Q. Were you surprised that she had your phone number?

A. No.

Q. Why not?

A. It is posted on my Web page.

Q. And what did you and Ms. Nobile discuss?

A. She tried to act tough and threatened me about consequences if I published a story about her and the judge.

Q. Oh? She doesn't strike me as the kind of person who goes around threatening other people.

A. You don't know your client very well, I guess.

Q. How many conversations did you have with Ms. Nobile after the one where you called her back?

A. Two or three.

Q. What were you discussing?

A. I did not really care much about her. She is a small fish. I wanted to get at the story about Elliot. So when she seemed so interested in keeping her name out of the news, she seemed willing to rat him out in exchange for keeping her name clean.

Q. Really? She suggested that she would, in your words, "rat out" the judge?

A. Yes.

Q. So you went back and forth over the course of a few phone calls trying to make a deal?

A. Yes, we did. And even though I had good sources, I gave her a couple of days to make up her mind. I should have known that she would slap me with the TRO to shut me up and try to kill the story.

Q. One more question, and I think that will be all: you are aware that if you threatened Ms. Nobile with publishing her name unless she gave you information about the judge that you could be guilty of extortion, aren't you?

MR. RUSSELL: Don't answer that. That is a threat of your own, Connell.

MS. CONNELL: Stop that Coop. That is a legal question that any good journalist would be able to answer. Isn't he sufficiently informed about the law?

MR. RUSSELL: Are you done?

MS. CONNELL: Yes. He is all yours. Oh, no, I am not. Mr. Ridge, I almost forgot a very important question. What are you going to say about Ms. Nobile in your article?

MR. RUSSELL: Don't answer that question. That goes to the merits of this case.

MS. CONNELL: Mr. Russell, it also goes to the New York long-arm statute, unless you are not relying on sub-section (a)(2) or (a)(3). If you want to waive that argument and just argue due process, be my guest. Otherwise, I am entitled to ask that question and some more as well.

MR. RUSSELL: Don't answer the question; don't say anything about the story.

MS. CONNELL: I will ask you one more time, Mr. Ridge, are you going to assert that Ms. Nobile knowingly possessed child pornography?

MR. RUSSELL: My instructions stand, Mike.

MS. CONNELL: Are you going to write she possessed the material in a way to let the reader assume that she possessed child pornography in some culpable manner?

MR. RUSSELL: Don't answer.

MS. CONNELL: We will be visiting with Judge Bricker. I would like to see if she is available today to get this resolved. Are you done?

MR. RUSSELL: No. But I won't be long. I have only a few questions. The first is this. You don't actually know that people in New York follow your blog and visit your Web site, do you?

A. I just assume so. The two states ...

Q. No, don't assume. You know that we deal with facts, not speculation. And visitors to MDC's Web site may have access to your Web site, but again, you don't have personal knowledge about that, do you?

A. That is right.

Q. And my last question before we end for the day. You never foresaw being haled into court in New York when you posted information on your website?

MS. CONNELL: Objection. That is irrelevant. It is a legal conclusion.

MR. RUSSELL: This is not the place for that debate. Answer the question, Mike.

A. I sure did not.

MS. CONNELL: I have a couple more questions.

MR. RUSSELL: I thought that we were done. I have other business to do.

MS. CONNELL: If this is not a good time, I will ask Judge Bricker to let us meet again. Your preference.

MR. RUSSELL: Get on with it.

MS. CONNELL: You are aware that Judge Elliot is rumored to be making a political comeback?

A. I have heard rumors.

Q. And you have heard his name mentioned as a possible U.S. Attorney or United States District judge, haven't you?

A. I have heard such musings. Those seem like pretty far-fetched stories though.

Q. But if true, would people outside Connecticut care about a USA or federal Judge watching kiddy pornography?

A. I guess so.

Q. You guess so? How many hits do you think a story about Senator Craig might have gotten?

MR. RUSSELL: That is not really a question, Mike. She is grandstanding. We are out of here.

MS. CONNELL: See you before Judge Bricker.

(Adjourned, noon, September 16, YR-00).

**REPORTER'S CERTIFICATE:**

I am a certified stenographic reporter in the State of Connecticut. I hereby certify that the foregoing deposition of Michael Ridge was taken before me at the time and place stated above, at which time the witness was placed under oath by me.

I hereby certify that the testimony of the witness and all objections made at the time of examination were recorded stenographically by me and were thereafter transcribed by me. I further certify that I am neither counsel nor related in any manner to any party to this action nor am I in any manner interested in the outcome thereof.

Sworn by me, September 30, YR-00.

*Ralph Lardner*
Ralph Lardner

In the United States District Court

for the

Central District of New York

| | | |
|---|---|---|
| Sarah D. Nobile,<br>Plaintiff<br>v.<br>Michael Ridge and<br>MDC, Inc.<br>Defendants | )<br>)<br>)<br>)<br>)<br>) | Civil Action No. 00–123 |

**DEPOSITION OF JOCELYN RAIDER**

Taken by Plaintiff, at Law Offices of Preston Pearson, Attorney at Law, Suite 9, the Frank Building, Dodd Plaza, Doddville, Connecticut, commencing at10:30 a.m., September 17, YR-00.

Appearances

For Plaintiff:

Adrian Connell
139 McGeorge Avenue
Cuomo City, New York 11774
(561) 782–1897

For Defendants:

R. Cooper Russell
Russell and Scott
Attorneys at Law
Suite 6
McGeorge Towers
Cuomo City, New York 11774
(561) 782–0099

Having been duly sworn, Jocelyn Raider testified as follows:

MS. CONNELL: Q. Good morning, Ms. Raider. For the record, Ms. Raider, you are represented by Mr. Russell, and you are aware that he also represents Michael Ridge, MDC, Inc.'s co-defendant?

A. I am aware of that fact.

Q. And has counsel, Mr. Russell, explained any possible conflict of interests that may arise?

A. Yes, to me and to other members of MDC.

Q. Would you begin by spelling your name for the record?

A. Jocelyn Raider, J–O–C–E–L–Y–N, R–A–I–D–E–R.

Q. Ms. Ridge, oh, I am sorry, Ms. Raider, is this your first deposition?

A. No.

Q. How often have you been deposed?

A. Several times. My employer has assigned me the job of testifying.

Q. In defamation cases?

A. Yes.

Q. Invasion of privacy?

A. Yes.

Q. You do understand the purpose of the deposition then?

A. Yes.

Q. You understand the court has entered an order allowing discovery on Ridge and MDC's motion in Nobile v. Ridge?

A. Yes.

Q. You do understand that you are under oath and that you may be prosecuted for perjury if you do not tell the truth?

A. Yes, I do understand that fact.

Q. Do you have reservations about telling the truth today?

A. No.

Q. Are you suffering from any impairment today that would not allow you to testify with accurately?

A. No.

Q. Would you tell me your educational background and qualifications?

A. In YR-13, I graduated from Southern Connecticut State University in business administration. Three years later, I received an MBA from State.

Q. And would you tell me about your employment history?

A. Yes. In YR-09, I went to work in the accounting department at MDC's parent company MDC, International.

Q. Wait a second. I am a little confused. Mr. Ridge is employed by MDC, Inc., isn't he?

A. Yes.

Q. But that is a separate entity from MDC, International?

A. Yes. (Directing her question to Mr. Russell), should I explain the connection?

MR. RUSSELL: Perhaps we could go off the record for a moment.

MS. CONNELL: If that will expedite this deposition, fine.

(After a short adjournment, questioning resumed).

MS. CONNELL: So, if you would briefly summarize what you stated moments ago?

A. Yes. MDC, Inc., my employer and defendant in this case is a subsidiary of MDC, International. MDC, International created a series of subsidiaries a few years ago.

Q. While you are not going to speculate about why the parent company did that, you explained the effect of that change in the company's structure?

A. Yes. As in a case like this, MDC, Inc. focuses almost exclusively on Connecticut news and politics. It hires investigative reporters like Mr. Ridge to concentrate on state government. It is a regional entity.

Q. But MDC, Inc. or its employees like you must know that a lot of folks in other states read anything that is published on the Web site. Isn't that true?

A. Maybe.

Q. Well, are you aware of how many people visit the website?

A. We have a good idea of how many hits we get, yes.

Q. Do you have any idea where the person is who goes to the website?

A. We do not.

Q. Is it possible to determine that?

A. It is, but we find it inaccurate and hence do not take the effort to review the result.

Q. Could you please confirm, you do have location information you choose not to look at?

A. That is correct; we find it inaccurate.

Q. Why do you believe this information to be inaccurate?

A. In general, the location information that we can generate determines where your ISP's hub is located. While this typically is regionally accurate for home users, for corporate users, this can be wherever the company has chosen to allow access to the Internet.

Q. Why would this not be an accurate reflection of your user's location?

A. Smartphones and corporate users cause the most headaches. Corporate users are more concerned about speed when accessing the Internet than home users, if solely due to bandwidth needs. As such, they choose to connect to the Internet where they can get the best connection. For the East Coast, that's a place called MAE–East. Once upon a time, it was a specific location in Virginia, but to improve service, they have added four additional locations, two in Virginia, one in Miami, and one in New York City. This results in many corporations connecting to the Internet in these locations, thus skewing the results in favor of these locations. In addition, with a MAE East node in New York City, many ISPs in the tri-state area (New York, New Jersey and Connecticut) have placed their "local" hubs in the same facility to speed access and to facilitate peering relationships.

Q. Why smartphones?

A. Smartphones roam. While many users will remain in the same geographic area, commuters are the problem. To access the Internet, a smartphone needs to be assigned an IP address, even if virtual within the carrier's system. Assigning the address requires allocating the resource (via DHCP), which requires overhead on the network. Because of the overhead, your IP address for your smartphone is deemed valid for a certain period of time, in many cases seven days. This address determines your location information. As you can imagine, that location for seven days will always report the location when the address was assigned, meaning it could be Connecticut, New Jersey, or New York, even if you live in Connecticut. If you go on a business trip, it may be the location you were when your address needed to be renewed ... so San Francisco for a week, despite being in Connecticut for six of those days.

Q. Please explain "peering relationships."

A. Most people assume that the Internet is one big giant cloud and that everyone shares. In fact, it's a series of clouds owned by ISPs such as Comcast, AT & T, BellSouth, Verizon, and hundreds of other companies. These ISPs are in essence tiered based on size and activities. The lowest tier, tier 1, handles the direct access to the end-user/corporation. They handle e-mail services, connection services, and direct support. Tier 2 providers provide regional/national services, provide co-location services (host servers that run Web sites). Finally Tier 3 providers are your national brands with large backbone implementations. Of course, providers in higher tiers may also provide services in lower tiers (e.g. AT & T providing home Internet services, yet they have a large national backbone). Each tier contracts with a higher tier provider to transmit their data. This contract has a cost. So if a Tier 2 provider finds that they have a lot of traffic going to another Tier 2 provider (or a tier 1 provider), they engage in peering, which is a direct connection between the two providers that neither provider is charged for. This is why locations like MAE East are so important, peering relationships can be handled with physical wires between the ISPs systems.

Q. Aren't these known issues that you can correct for?

A. Yes, but its value is not worth the cost to us.

Q. But companies like Google provide targeted ads based on location, the same location data you feel is skewed, why not use location data?

A. We aren't in the same business.

Q. Does Google sell ads?

A. To the best of my knowledge, yes.

Q. Does MDC, Inc. sell ads?

A. Yes.

Q. Then how are you not in the same business?

A. Google is selling ads for a national audience attempting to deliver ads that are tailored to the viewer based on their recent activities across all of their sites and on location. That provides a tailored ad to each viewer. We do not have access to the level of personal data about our viewers that Google does. However, we know at MDC, Inc., our content is focused on Connecticut politicians, so we sell our ads based on interest in Connecticut politicians. So a different business, we maintain one Web site, not hundreds with a unified login.

Q. But you could determine their location if you chose to do so?

A. Yes.

Q. MDC, Inc. hosts a public Web site or Web sites, correct?

A. Yes, that's true.

Q. So people anywhere in the world can access the pages that you host and find stories that are posted there; that is also correct, isn't it?

A. Yes.

Q. Where are your servers located?

A. Fairfield County, Connecticut.

Q. Who hosts your servers?

A. Cervalis, Inc.

Q. Do you have any servers not located with Cervalis, Inc.?

A. No, they host all of MDC, Inc.'s servers.

Q. Apart from the Internet and Web, what marketing efforts does MDC, Inc. undertake?

A. MDC, Inc. helps sponsor an annual blogger event put on by CTWeblogs.com to help people improve the quality of blogs focused on Connecticut. It's a one day event held at the Sheraton in Stamford, CT each year.

Q. That's all of your marketing efforts?

A. That is all of our non-Internet marketing.

Q. What Internet marketing efforts do you undertake?

A. We purchase various Web ads on various sites interested in Connecticut politics.

Q. Do you purchase location related ads from Google?

A. Yes.

Q. What are your criteria for those ads?

A. Connecticut, politician, corruption, Hartford, general assembly.

Q. Do you limit viewer's locations?

A. Yes, due to the problem with skewing due to corporations and smartphones, we feel we cannot limit our ads solely to Connecticut, so we limit our ads to Connecticut, Rhode Island, New York, New Jersey, and Massachusetts.

Q. So you advertise to New York residents?

A. To the extent they are searching for Connecticut political news, we do not stop ads from being shown to New York residents, but we don't believe we are targeting New York residents, simply allowing for the shortcomings of Internet location determination.

Q. How long do you retain your logs?

A. We retain our error logs for 90 days. Our traffic logs for one year. Beyond that we retain permanently monthly summary reports.

Q. Have you answered each of the prior questions completely?

A. Yes.

Q. Is there anything you'd like to add to any response?

A. No.

Q. Thank you for your time today.

A. You're welcome.

**REPORTER'S CERTIFICATE:**

I am a certified stenographic reporter in the State of Connecticut. I hereby certify that the foregoing deposition of Michael Ridge was taken before me at the time and place stated above, at which time the witness was placed under oath by me.

I hereby certify that the testimony of the witness and all objections made at the time of examination were recorded steno-graphically by me and were thereafter transcribed by me. I further certify that I am neither counsel nor related in any manner to any party to this action nor am I in any manner interested in the outcome thereof.

Sworn by me, October 1, YR-00.

*Ralph Lardner*
Ralph Lardner

# CHAPTER THREE

# SUBJECT MATTER JURISDICTION (DIVERSITY)

## I. INTRODUCTION

As you saw in Chapter Two, the plaintiff filed her action in federal court and the defendants contested the court's personal jurisdiction. Assume that the court denied the defendants' motion to dismiss for lack of personal jurisdiction. Still intent on getting the case dismissed, Defendant Ridge questions whether the court has subject matter jurisdiction over the dispute.

This chapter includes two simulations along with a series of study questions. The first part of the chapter focuses on diversity jurisdiction. The second simulation expands the discussion to include questions about supplemental jurisdiction in diversity actions. The second exercise includes an amended complaint with the addition of a co-plaintiff.

## II. DIVERSITY

Earlier, you learned that Sarah Nobile rents an apartment in Cuomo City, New York, but has kept her condominium in Doddville, Connecticut. Meanwhile her husband lives in Cuomo City. Once counsel for Michael Ridge learned those facts, he wonders whether Ms. Nobile remains a citizen of Connecticut. If so, the court would lack subject matter jurisdiction because Mr. Ridge is a citizen of Connecticut.

Review the Plaintiff's Complaint and the Defendants' motion to dismiss in Chapter Two. You will notice the absence of a challenge to the court's subject matter jurisdiction. Does counsel's failure to raise the issue waive the objection to the court's subject matter jurisdiction? Read F.R.C.P. 12(b)(1) and F.R.C.P. 12(h)(3). Consider why the rules handle objections to subject matter jurisdiction as they do.

On the assumption that Mr. Ridge's attorney decides to challenge the court's subject matter jurisdiction, other than filing a motion, how should counsel proceed? Are the Plaintiff's allegations about her citizenship entitled to any weight? How can counsel for the Defendant overcome her allegations in her complaint? Rule 12 provides relatively little guidance on the latter question. See F.R.C.P. 12(i).[1]

---

1. A similar problem arises when a defendant challenges the assertion of personal jurisdiction. Reexamine Chapter Two to see one option a court has.

After considering those questions, examine the cases in your casebook. See if those cases explain how the courts developed the record. Given the lack of clear guidance on how litigants are to build the factual record under the rules, how should the litigants do so in this case?

Arguably, Defendant Ridge has yet to cause any harm to Ms. Nobile.[2] At a minimum, the harm she has already experienced is fairly minor. In light of that fact, does her complaint satisfy the jurisdictional amount? How should a court value an injunction? Does the injunction have the same value to the plaintiff and to the defendant?[3]

Your professor has some option on how to handle this simulation. One option is to use the questions posed in this chapter as the basis of a classroom discussion. Alternatively, your professor may assign students various roles, including the role of Ms. Nobile, and conduct an evidentiary hearing on the issues developed above.

# III. SUPPLEMENTAL JURISDICTION

## A. Some Study Questions

In her original action, Ms. Nobile was the only plaintiff. Under the substantive law of most states, her husband may bring a claim for loss of consortium.[4] Consider the strategic advantages of adding her husband as a co-plaintiff. Examine the Federal Rules of Civil Procedure to determine whether her husband can (or must) join as a co-party.

Assume that Ms. Nobile and her attorney have filed an amended complaint, adding her husband, Nick Rossi, as a co-plaintiff. Here is the amended complaint, followed by additional questions:

---

**2.** That point is arguable because she has experienced some emotional harm from Ridge's threat to publish the story.

**3.** An example from Freer and Perdue's casebook makes the point: if a defendant has constructed a building encroaching on the plaintiff's property, the plaintiff's loss of a small piece of her property may be less than the jurisdictional amount. But if the court were to order the defendant to tear down the building, the amount in controversy would satisfy the jurisdictional amount.

**4.** As defined by one court, "[A]lthough loss of consortium is a separate cause of action, it is an action [which] is derivative of the injured spouse's cause of action.... Loss of consortium, although a separate cause of action, is not truly independent, but rather derivative and inextricably attached to the claim of the injured spouse" ... The definition of the term "consortium" includes spousal services, financial support and "the variety of intangible relations which exist between spouses living together in marriage.... These intangible elements are generally described in terms of 'affection, society, companionship and sexual relations.' ... These intangibles have also been defined as the 'constellation of companionship, dependence, reliance, affection, sharing and aid which are legally recognizable, protected rights arising out of the civil contract of marriage.'" *Connecticut Ins. Guar. Ass'n v. Fontaine,* 900 A.2d 18 (Conn. 2006).

## B. The Amended Complaint

In the United States District Court

for the

Central District of New York

| | | |
|---|---|---|
| Sarah D. Nobile, and | ) | |
| Nick Rossi | ) | |
| Plaintiffs | ) | Civil Action No. 00–123 |
| v. | ) | |
| Michael Ridge; and | ) | |
| MDC, Inc. | ) | |
| Defendants | ) | |

### COMPLAINT FOR INJUNCTIVE RELIEF AND FOR DAMAGES FOR DEFAMATION AND INVASION OF PRIVACY

Plaintiffs Sarah D. Nobile and Nick Rossi, on personal knowledge as to their acts, and on information and belief as to all others based on its investigation, allege as follows:

### INTRODUCTION

1. Plaintiffs, Sarah D. Nobile and Nick Rossi, bring this action to prevent Defendant Michael Ridge from publishing a story that the Defendant knows to be false and misleading, putting Plaintiff Nobile in a false light and that will damage her irreparably. The Plaintiffs join as co-Defendant MDC, Inc., Defendant Ridge's employer.

### STATEMENT OF JURISDICTION

2. Plaintiffs are citizens of the State of New York. Defendant Michael Ridge is a citizen of the State of Connecticut. Defendant MDC, Inc. is a citizen of Delaware, its state of incorporation, and Connecticut, its principal place of business.

3. The amount in controversy, without interest and costs, exceeds the sum or value specified in 28 U.S.C. § 1332.

### FACTUAL BACKGROUND

4. On August 28, YR-05, Plaintiff Nobile began working for Connecticut State Judge John Elliot.

5. During her period of employment for Judge Elliot, Plaintiff Nobile worked in Judge Elliot's Chambers in the Appellate Court Building, 123 Nutley Avenue, Harford, Connecticut.

6. As part of her job, Plaintiff Nobile was assigned a workstation in an office shared with Judge Elliot's other law clerk, Nathan Loewe.

7. Plaintiff Nobile's workstation included a Dell Computer, with access to the Internet, which she was allowed to use to conduct legal research on various legal data bases.

8. At all times, Plaintiff Nobile followed office policy and used her computer for proper business purposes only.

9. On June 1, YR-03, members of Doddville City Police Department [Police Department, hereinafter] executed a search warrant for Judge Elliot's chambers.

10. During the course of the search, a member of the Police Department removed two computers from Judge Elliot's chambers.

11. On June 10, YR-03, a technician working for the Police Department, allegedly found child pornography on two of the computers, including Plaintiff Nobile's.

12. Because of serious questions about the legality of the warrant and because many other people had access to the computers, the Doddville District Attorney's Office refused to prosecute Plaintiff Nobile.

13. For reasons stated in Paragraph 12, the Doddville District Attorney Clara Saint-Jean agreed to seal the warrant because of concerns that revealing information about the search would unfairly damage Plaintiff Nobile's and others' reputations.

14. On August 3, YR-00, Plaintiff Nobile received a phone call from Judge Elliot's former secretary, Rhoda Sheen, who told her that Defendant Michael Ridge was threatening to publish an article claiming that Plaintiff Nobile and Judge Elliot were guilty of possessing child pornography on their office computers.

15. Also on August 3, YR-00, with the hope of stopping the publication of a false and defamatory story, Plaintiff Nobile called Defendant Ridge and left a voicemail in which she told him of her concerns.

16. Defendant Ridge called Plaintiff Nobile on August 4, YR-00 and told her that he was going to name her in the story and post it on his Blog GOTCHA! He also told her that the main focus of the story was Judge Elliot, whom Defendant Ridge called a hypocrite, and intimated that if Plaintiff Nobile would be a source confirming the facts in the story about the Judge, he would delete her name.

17. Plaintiff Nobile begged for time to consider what to do. She brings this suit to stop publication of a false and defamatory article that may go "viral" on the Internet, permanently harming her reputation.

**COUNT ONE**

18. Paragraphs 4-17 are hereby incorporated by reference. Defendant Ridge's story alleging that Plaintiff Nobile possessed child pornography is false and defamatory.

## COUNT TWO

19. Paragraphs 4-17 are hereby incorporated by reference. Defendant Ridge's story alleging that Plaintiff Nobile possessed child pornography violates her right to privacy. Specifically, even a statement limited to the fact that child pornography was found on her computer puts Plaintiff Nobile in a false light.

## COUNT THREE

20. Paragraphs 4-17 are hereby incorporated by reference. Defendant MDC, Inc. is liable to Plaintiff Nobile under the theory of respondeat superior as Defendant Ridge's employer.

## COUNT FOUR

21. Paragraphs 4-17 are hereby incorporated by reference. Defendant Ridge is liable to Plaintiff Rossi for the loss of consortium due to the suffering he is causing Plaintiff Nobile.

## COUNT FIVE

22. Paragraphs 4-17 are hereby incorporated by reference. Defendant MDC, Inc. is liable to Plaintiff Rossi for the loss of consortium under the theory of respondeat superior as Defendant Ridge's employer.

## PRAYER FOR RELIEF

23. Plaintiffs request that this Court temporarily during the pendency of this action restrain Defendant Ridge and all persons acting in concert with Defendant Ridge from publishing or otherwise disseminating any story concerning Plaintiff Nobile that alleges that child pornography was found on her computer or in any other way linking her to illegal activity based on the search of Judge Elliot's chambers.

24. Plaintiffs request that this Court enjoin Defendant Ridge and all persons acting in concert with Defendant Ridge from publishing or otherwise disseminating any story concerning Plaintiff Nobile that alleges that child pornography was found on her computer or in any other way linking her to illegal activity based on the search of Judge Elliot's chambers.

25. Plaintiffs request that this Court temporarily during the pendency of this action and permanently enjoin Defendant Ridge from publishing or disseminating in any manner a copy of the search warrant issued for the search of Judge Elliot's office dated May 26, YR-03 or any information learned from examination of that document.

26. Plaintiffs request that this Court temporarily during the pendency of this action and permanently enjoin Defendant Ridge from publishing or disseminating in any manner a copy of any other documents relating to the search warrant issued for the search of Judge Elliot's office dated May 26, YR-03 or any information learned from examination of those documents, including but not limited to the Affidavit of Probable Cause and the Return on the Warrant.

27. Plaintiffs request compensatory damages in such amount as the court shall determine to compensate Plaintiffs for their damages suffered as a result of Defendant Ridge's conduct. They request that the Court enter judgment for those damages against Defendant Ridge and/or Defendant MDC, Inc.

28. Plaintiffs request punitive damages in such amount as the court shall determine to punish Defendant Ridge for his outrageous and unlawful conduct. They request that the Court enter judgment for those damages against Defendant Ridge and/or Defendant MDC, Inc.

29. Plaintiffs request their costs of suit and reasonable attorneys' fees;

30. Plaintiffs request such other relief to which they may be entitled.

Respectfully submitted,

*Adrian Connell*

Adrian Connell
139 McGeorge Avenue
Cuomo City, New York 11774
(561) 782–1897

Dated: August 6, YR-00

## C. Additional Study Questions

Your professor may assign students the job of making a formal argument before the court on the jurisdictional questions posed in this exercise. Alternatively, your professor may use this material and the questions below for an in-class discussion of supplemental jurisdiction.

Section 1332 limits diversity actions to suits for an amount in excess of $75,000. What if the Defendants want to challenge the jurisdictional amount? Consider how they do so and which party has the burden of showing that the amount does or does not exceed the jurisdictional amount.

Earlier, you considered whether Ms. Nobile's claim exceeded that amount. Assume that it did not. Could the plaintiffs aggregate their claims against the Defendants?

Assume that Ms. Nobile's claim does exceed the jurisdictional amount.[5] Assume further that the Defendants want to challenge her joinder of her husband's claim on the ground that his claim fails to satisfy the jurisdictional amount.[6] Even if his claim did fail to exceed $75,000, would the court have supplemental jurisdiction over Rossi's claim under § 1367?

---

**5.** Case law suggests that defendants seldom can prevail if they challenge the jurisdictional amount when the plaintiff's claim is for unliquidated tort damages.

**6.** As indicated earlier, such an argument is not likely to prevail because his claim, like his wife's involves unliquidated tort damages. But imagine a case in which a defendant could show that the married couple were contemplating a divorce or were otherwise not happily married, thereby limiting any claim that the spouse might have for loss of consortium.

Assume the complaint named Ridge as the only defendant and the defendant proved that Rossi is a citizen of Connecticut. Does the court have supplemental jurisdiction over Rossi's claim under § 1367?

# CHAPTER FOUR

# SUBJECT MATTER JURISDICTION (FEDERAL QUESTION) AND REMOVAL

## I. INTRODUCTION

As you saw earlier, Ms. Nobile filed her action in a federal district court in New York. In Chapter 3, the court had to decide whether the Plaintiff was a citizen of New York or Connecticut. Assume that the court found that she was a citizen of Connecticut and, therefore, dismissed the action. Assume that the court kept in place the injunction for three days to give the Plaintiff time to re-file her action. As a result, Ms. Nobile and her attorney filed an action against Mr. Ridge in New York state court and this action in Connecticut state court.

Ms. Nobile and her attorney face some strategic problems. For example, they have not been able to identify Ridge's source of his information about the raid and sealed search warrant. They have only a hunch about possible sources, including Ms. Nobile's former co-clerk, Nathan Loewe. They need to name Loewe as a co-defendant if he is the source, but cannot do so without some basis for their allegation. See F.R.C.P. 11(b)(3) ("an attorney ... certifies that ... the factual contentions have evidentiary support or, if specifically so identified, will likely have evidentiary support after a reasonable opportunity for further investigation or discovery; ...") They face a different problem with regard to naming specific police officers who may have revealed information under seal to Ridge. At this point, they have no idea who may have been involved.

As discussed in more detail in the next section, assume that Ms. Nobile filed an action against named defendants along with unnamed police officers in the Doddville Police Department as defendants in state court. Also assume that the named defendants removed the action to federal court. This chapter introduces you to several important concepts, including federal question jurisdiction, supplemental jurisdiction, and removal. Section II discusses Ms. Nobile and her attorney's decision to file the action in state court. Section III contains the complaint filed in that action. Section IV discusses the Defendants' strategy. Section V consists of the Defendants' Notice of Removal; Section VI includes the Plaintiff's Motion for Remand. Finally, Section VII discusses the simulation exercises that your professor may assign in connection with this material.

## II. THE LAWSUIT: SOME BACKGROUND

Ms. Nobile and her attorney have decided to file suit against unnamed police officers for violating Ms. Nobile's constitutional rights. She has based her claim on 42 U.S.C. § 1983.[1] As reflected in her complaint, her theory is that the police violated her Fourth Amendment rights to be free from an unreasonable search when Doddville police officers searched the Judge's chambers and her computer. In addition, they want to add claims against the police for leaking the information to Mr. Ridge. As she alleges in her complaint, that conduct amounts to an invasion of her privacy. In part because she and her attorney have not been able to learn who leaked the information to Ridge, they have also added as a co-defendant Nathan Loewe, whom they have some reason to believe may have been involved. Even though she has a pending action against Mr. Ridge in state court in New York, she has joined him as a co-defendant in this action as well.

Ms. Connell decided to add the state law claims against the police officers for a number of reasons. Suing a municipality for a violation of § 1983 has an interesting history: until 1978, the Supreme Court held that Congress intended to exempt municipalities from suit under § 1983. In 1978, it reversed itself, but limited a plaintiff's ability to recover against such entities. Section 1983 requires more than a showing of vicarious liability for the acts of, for example, the municipality's police officers. Instead, a plaintiff must show a formal policy, governmental custom, inadequate training or supervision, or inadequate hiring before she can prevail against the municipality. But assume that under state law, the officers' employer is liable under respondeat superior if the officers committed a tort.

The next section includes Ms. Nobile's state law complaint.

---

1. Section 1983 provides in relevant part: "Every person who, under color of any statute, ordinance, regulation, custom, or usage, of any State or Territory or the District of Columbia, subjects, or causes to be subjected, any citizen of the United States or other person within the jurisdiction thereof to the deprivation of any rights, privileges, or immunities secured by the Constitution and laws, shall be liable to the party injured in an action at law, suit in equity, or other proper proceeding for redress, except that in any action brought against a judicial officer for an act or omission taken in such officer's judicial capacity, injunctive relief shall not be granted unless a declaratory decree was violated or declaratory relief was unavailable."

# III. THE LAWSUIT: THE COMPLAINT[2]

Superior Court of Connecticut

County of Doddville

| | | |
|---|---|---|
| Sarah D. Nobile,<br>Plaintiff<br>v.<br>Department of Police for<br>The City of Doddville;<br>MDC, Inc.; Nathan Loewe;<br>Michael Ridge; and<br>Unnamed Officers of<br>The DPCCD;<br>Defendants | )<br>)<br>)<br>)<br>)<br>)<br>)<br>)<br>)<br>) | No. 00–34–1689 |

## COMPLAINT

Plaintiff Sarah D. Nobile, on personal knowledge as to her own acts, and on information and belief as to all others based on its investigation, alleges as follows:

### NATURE OF THE ACTION

1. Plaintiff, Sarah D. Nobile, brings this action against the above-captioned defendants for violating her constitutional right to be free from an unreasonable search; for conspiring to violate her constitutional right to be free from an unreasonable search; for violating her right to privacy; and for conspiring to violate her right to privacy.

### FACTUAL BACKGROUND

2. On August 28, YR-05, Plaintiff began working for Connecticut State Judge John Elliot.

3. During her period of employment for Judge Elliot, Plaintiff worked in Judge Elliot's Chambers in the Appellate Court Building, 123 Nutley Avenue, Hartford, Connecticut.

4. As part of her job, Plaintiff was assigned a workstation in an office shared with Judge Elliot's other law clerk, Defendant Nathan Loewe.

5. Plaintiff's workstation included a Dell Computer, with access to the Internet, which she was allowed to use to conduct legal research on various legal data bases.

6. At all times, Plaintiff followed office policy and used her computer for proper business purposes only.

7. On June 1, YR-03, Defendants unnamed members of Doddville City Police Department executed a search warrant for Judge Elliot's chambers.

---

2. Along with this complaint, the Plaintiff filed a motion for a temporary restraining order, which the state court granted.

8. During the course of the search, a member of the Police Department removed two computers from Judge Elliot's chambers.

9. On June 10, YR-03, a technician working for the Defendant Police Department, allegedly found child pornography on two of the computers, including Plaintiff's.

10. Because of serious questions about the legality of the warrant and because many other people had access to the computers, the Doddville District Attorney's Office refused to prosecute Plaintiff.

11. For reasons stated in Paragraph 10, the Doddville District Attorney Clara Saint-Jean agreed to seal the warrant because of concerns that revealing information about the search would unfairly damage Plaintiff's and others' reputations.

12. At some time prior to August 3, YR-00, one or more of the individual Defendants (Nathan Loewe or one of the unnamed police officers) leaked information about the contents of the sealed search warrant to Defendant Michael Ridge.

13. On August 3, YR-00, Plaintiff received a phone call from Judge Elliot's former secretary, Rhoda Sheen, who told her that Defendant Michael Ridge was threatening to publish an article claiming that Plaintiff and Judge Elliot were guilty of possessing child pornography on their office computers.

14. Also on August 3, YR-00, with the hope of stopping the publication of a false and defamatory story, Plaintiff called Defendant Ridge and left a voicemail in which she told him of her concerns.

15. Defendant Ridge called Plaintiff on August 4, YR-00 and told her that he was going to name her in the story and post it on his blog, GOTCHA! He also told her that the main focus of the story was Judge Elliot, whom Defendant Ridge called a hypocrite, and intimated that if Plaintiff would be a source confirming the facts in the story about the Judge, he would delete her name.

16. Plaintiff begged for time to consider what to do. In an effort to stop publication of a false and defamatory article that may go "viral" on the Internet, permanently harming her reputation, Plaintiff filed an action in United States District Court for the Central District of New York on August 6, YR-00. On August 7, YR-00, that court entered an order temporarily enjoining Defendants Ridge and MDC, Inc. from publishing in any medium, including but not limited to books, newspapers, magazines, radio, television or any site on the Internet or World Wide Web, disseminating or in any other manner disclosing information learned from the sealed documents implicating Plaintiff in criminal activity.

17. On September 26, YR-00, that court entertained a preliminary injunction barring Defendants Ridge and MDC, Inc. from publishing in any medium, including but not limited to books, newspapers, magazines, radio, television or any site on the Internet or World Wide Web, disseminating or in any other manner disclosing information learned from the sealed documents implicating Plaintiff in criminal activity.

## COUNT ONE

18. Paragraphs 2-17 are hereby incorporated by reference. Defendants Unnamed Officers violated the Plaintiff's Fourth Amendment right to be free from an unreasonable search. Their conduct violated Plaintiff's rights protected by 42 U.S.C. § 1983.

## COUNT TWO

19. Paragraphs 2-17 are hereby incorporated by reference. Defendants Unnamed Officers, Defendant Nathan Loewe, and Defendant Michael Ridge are liable to Plaintiff for violating her rights of privacy protected by Connecticut law. That conspiracy resulted in Defendant Ridge learning of private information learned through the illegal search of her computer.

## COUNT THREE

20. Paragraphs 2-17 are hereby incorporated by reference. Defendant MDC, Inc. is liable to Plaintiff under the theory of respondeat superior as Defendant Ridge's employer.

## COUNT FOUR

21. Paragraphs 2-17 are hereby incorporated by reference. Defendant Department of Police for the City of Doddville is liable to Plaintiff under the theory of respondeat superior as Defendant Unnamed Officers' employer.

## PRAYER FOR RELIEF

22. Plaintiff requests that this Court enjoin all of the Defendants and all persons acting in concert with Defendants from publishing or otherwise disseminating any information concerning allegations child pornography that was found on Plaintiff's computer or in any other way linking her to illegal activity based on the search of Judge Elliot's chambers.

23. Plaintiff requests damages in such amount as the court shall determine to compensate Plaintiff for her damages suffered as a result of Defendants conduct.

24. Plaintiff requests punitive damages in such amount as the court shall determine to punish Defendants for their outrageous and unlawful conduct.

25. Plaintiff requests her costs of suit and reasonable attorneys' fees;

26. Plaintiff requests such other relief to which she may be entitled.

Respectfully submitted,

*Adrian Connell*
Adrian Connell
139 McGeorge Avenue
Cuomo City, New York 11774
(561) 782–1897

Dated: September 30, YR-00

## IV. THE DEFENDANTS' STRATEGY

As you have seen in earlier chapters, forum-shopping matters. Factors that influence where litigants want to try their cases vary widely over time and from region to region. You may have studied *World-wide Volkswagen v. Woodson,* 444 U.S. 286 (1980). There, the parties fought vigorously about whether an Oklahoma state court had personal jurisdiction over two New York defendants (Seaway, the seller of an Audi, and its distributor, World–Wide Volkswagen). While the case created important Supreme Court precedent dealing with personal jurisdiction, the parties cared little about that issue. Audi and Volkswagen of America wanted to remove the action from state to federal court, something they could not do unless the New York defendants were dismissed. Local state courts tended to be friendlier to plaintiffs than did the big city federal courts.

Examples like this are common. The factors influencing forum-shopping are numerous and may not be visible to casual observers. Growing up in an era of liberal activist federal judges, lawyers of my generation thought of federal courts as friendly places for plaintiffs. That changed over time as Presidents Reagan, George H.W. Bush, and George W. Bush appointed a large number of conservative judges to the federal bench. Plaintiff may now prefer locally elected populist state court judges. Further, defendants seem to know what they are doing when they choose to remove from state to federal court. One empirical study found that plaintiffs win far less often in federal court when the defendant has removed the action than when the plaintiff chose federal court in the first instance.[3]

Other factors, like location of the court, state vs. federal rules, and the length of the trial docket, influence forum shopping as well. Thus, in the simulation, Ms. Nobile and her attorney may have had many reasons to file the action in state court. But the defendants may be able to negate Ms. Nobile's forum shopping by removing the action from state to federal court. At this point, examine § 1441, § 1446 and § 1447. Can the defendants remove the action, and if so, under which provision of § 1441? Sections 1446 and 1447 set forth the procedures applicable to removal.

---

3. See Clermont and Eisenberg, *Do Case Outcomes Really Reveal Anything About the Legal System? Win Rates and Removal Jurisdiction,* 83 Cornell L. Rev. 581 (1998) ("... overall win rate in federal cases is 57.97%, but in the subset of those cases that have been removed the win rate is only 36.77%.")

# V. THE DEFENDANTS' NOTICE OF REMOVAL TO FEDERAL COURT

In the United States District Court

for the District of Connecticut

| | | |
|---|---|---|
| Sarah D. Nobile, | ) | |
| Plaintiff | ) | No. 00–34–1689 |
| v. | ) | |
| Department of Police for | ) | |
| The City of Doddville; | ) | |
| MDC, Inc.; Nathan Loewe; | ) | |
| Michael Ridge; and | ) | |
| Unnamed Officers of | ) | |
| The DPCCD; | ) | |
| Defendants | ) | |

TO: THE JUDGES FOR THE UNITED STATES DISTRICT COURT FOR THE DISTRICT OF CONNECTICUT AND COUNSEL OF RECORD FOR THE PLAINTIFF, SARAH D. NOBILE

PLEASE TAKE NOTE that the Defendants in the above-titled matter hereby remove to this Court the state court action reflected in the attached pleading filed in the Superior Court for the County of Doddville in the State of Connecticut where it was pending.

RECORD IN THE STATE COURT: The following pleadings, as are available in the file of the state court action, encompass all of the pleadings received or filed by the Defendants in this action up to the present time: Summons, Complaint, Proof of Service and Notice of Appearance on Behalf of Defendants. The Complaint is attached hereto as Exhibit A.[4]

**THIS COURT'S SUBJECT MATTER JURISDICTION:** This dispute is based on allegations that Defendants Unnamed Police Officers of the DPCCD violated the Plaintiff's constitutional right to be free from an unreasonable search. See 42 U.S.C. § 1983. While the complaint also raises state law claims, this Court has subject matter jurisdiction over additional claims and parties because the Defendants are diverse from the Plaintiff and/or this Court has subject matter over those additional claims and parties under § 1367 or § 1441(c).

**CONCURRENT NOTICE TO STATE COURT:** Defendants are concurrently filing a copy of this Notice of Removal with the Clerk of Court of the Superior Court for the County of Doddville, State of Connecticut, case number 00–34–1689, pursuant to 28 U.S.C. § 1446(d).

**DATED** this 23 day of October, YR-00.

---

**4.** Assume that the Defendants have attached these documents as an appendix to their notice of removal.

Filed on behalf of all named defendants by

*R. Cooper Russell*

R. Cooper Russell
Russell and Scott
Attorneys at Law
Suite 6
McGeorge Towers
Cuomo City, New York 11774

**CERTIFICATE OF SERVICE**

I hereby certify that on October 23, YR-00, I electronically filed the following documents with the Clerk of the Court using the CM/ECF system that will send notification of such filing to Adrian Connell, Esquire; 139 McGeorge Avenue, Cuomo City, New York 11774.

*R. Cooper Russell*

R. Cooper Russell
Russell and Scott
Attorneys at Law
Suite 6
McGeorge Towers
Cuomo City, New York 11774

# VI. PLAINTIFF'S MOTION TO REMAND

In the United States District Court

for the District of Connecticut

| | | |
|---|---|---|
| Sarah D. Nobile, | ) | |
| Plaintiff | ) | No. 00–34–1689 |
| v. | ) | |
| Department of Police for | ) | |
| The City of Doddville; | ) | |
| MDC, Inc.; Nathan Loewe; | ) | |
| Michael Ridge; and | ) | |
| Unnamed Officers of | ) | |
| The DPCCD; | ) | |
| Defendants | ) | |

**PLAINTIFF'S MOTION TO REMAND**

The Plaintiff respectfully moves this Court to issue an order remanding this civil suit to the Superior Court for the County of Doddville, State of Connecticut.

1. On August 6, YR-00, the Plaintiff filed an action naming as Defendants Michael Ridge and his employer MDC, Inc. in the United States District Court in the Central District of New York.

2. On September 28, YR-00, after holding an evidentiary hearing, Judge John J. Leach found that the Plaintiff was a citizen of Connecticut and dismissed her action for lack of diversity.

3. On September 30, YR-00, the Plaintiff filed an action against the above named Defendants for violating her civil rights as well as for conspiring to violate her right to privacy.

4. On October 23, YR-00, the Defendants filed a Notice of Removal to this Court.

5. The Plaintiff now moves this Court to remand her action to state court. As grounds for this motion, the Plaintiff has attached[5] her amended complaint, deleting any claim arising under federal law.

6. Because the Plaintiff has been found to be a citizen of Connecticut and because the Defendants are citizens of Connecticut, this Court lacks subject matter jurisdiction over all of the state law claims alleged in the Plaintiff's Complaint.

---

**5.** Rather than replicating the complaint from above, assume that the Plaintiff has deleted the § 1983 claim, but otherwise makes the same claims against the same defendants.

7. Because this Court lacks subject matter based on either 28 U.S.C. § 1331 or § 1332, this Court must remand this action to the Superior Court for the County of Doddville, State of Connecticut.

Respectfully submitted,

*Adrian Connell*

Adrian Connell
139 McGeorge Avenue
Cuomo City, New York 11774
(561) 782–1897

October 28, YR-00

**CERTIFICATE OF SERVICE**

I hereby certify that on October 28, YR-00, I electronically filed the aforementioned documents with the Clerk of the Court using the CM/ECF system that will send notification of such filing to R. Cooper Russell, Esquire, Russell and Scott, Attorneys at Law, Suite 6, McGeorge Towers, Cuomo City, New York 11774.

*Adrian Connell*

Adrian Connell
139 McGeorge Avenue
Cuomo City, New York 11774
(561) 782–1897

October 28, YR-00

## VII. THE SIMULATION

As discussed above, the Plaintiff and Defendants are engaged in forum-shopping. Whether one side or the other prevails depends on a number of questions. Consider the section of § 1441 that allowed this action to be removed. The question is intentionally a close one and both the Plaintiff and Defendants can made good arguments to support their side of the issue. Further, whether the federal court should remand all or part of the action may depend on how it rules on the question this problem poses. Not only does this simulation introduce you to § 1441, but it also allows you to study § 1367, providing for supplemental jurisdiction. In studying § 1367, consider not only whether it creates subject matter jurisdiction over the non-diverse state law claims; consider also whether the court should use its discretion to remand part of the case to state court.

Your professor has a number of options when s/he assigns this chapter. For example, you may be assigned the role of counsel for the Plaintiff or the Defendants and asked to argue whether the Court should grant the Plaintiff's

Motion to Remand. Alternatively, s/he may have you write a short memorandum to the judge before whom the matter is pending, in which you explain how the Court should resolve this dispute.

# CHAPTER FIVE

# VENUE AND TRANSFER OF VENUE

## I. INTRODUCTION

Before filing suit, a plaintiff's attorney should consider a variety of factors, many of which are pragmatic, some of which are legal. Counsel may be able to file suit in more than one state and she may be able to choose between federal and state court. Often reasons to choose between one or the other depends on practical considerations (e.g., the state court is nearby while the federal court is in a remote city; the docket for the state court moves more slowly than the federal docket; federal discovery rules are more helpful to building a plaintiff's case than are the state rules). Counsel should also consider at least three legal questions as part of her pretrial forum shopping: notably, will the court in which the action is filed have personal jurisdiction over the defendant(s); if the plaintiff wants to sue in federal court, will the court have subject matter jurisdiction over the plaintiff's claim; and finally, is this a proper venue? Failing to satisfy any one of those requirements may lead to the plaintiff's action being dismissed.

This chapter focuses on related concepts of venue and transfer of venue. It does so within the federal system.[1] On the assumption that the plaintiff wants to sue in federal court, she must ask where within the federal system she should file her action. In the simulation, Ms. Nobile has decided to file in a federal district in New York. Before filing the action, her attorney should consider whether the case comes within the primary venue statute, § 1391.

Given the reality that a plaintiff has engaged in forum shopping prior to filing her action, not surprisingly, a defendant may find the forum a poor one. After all, a plaintiff may have chosen the forum because it is convenient for her and inconvenient for the defendant. She may have chosen it because of more favorable law than would apply in an alternative forum. She may have chosen it because juries give large damage awards, whereas had she filed elsewhere, juries may give small damage awards. As a result, a defendant may seek to frustrate the plaintiff's choice of the forum and do some forum shopping of his own.

This chapter consists of a brief discussion of venue and change of venue. Thereafter, it consists of a series of questions the litigants should consider in

---

1. States typically have their own venue statutes, sometimes quite complex with proper venue dependent on the nature of a plaintiff's claim. While federal law includes some specialized venue provisions, this chapter and most basic Civil Procedure courses deal with the basic venue statute.

arguing whether venue is proper in the United States District Court of the Central District of New York, why that matters, and whether transfer to a federal district in Connecticut would make sense. Finally, it includes a simulation exercise dealing with venue and transfer of venue.

## II. VENUE AND TRANSFER OF VENUE

As you saw in Chapter Two, Ms. Nobile filed her action in federal court and the Defendants contested the court's personal jurisdiction. The Defendants' motion to dismiss stated that venue was improper as well. In discussing the options available to the Defendants under the F.R.C.P., you have already recognized that not only did they have the option of joining their venue challenge in their original motion, but also that they would have waived the challenge had they not brought it along with the personal jurisdictional challenge. But what must the Defendants demonstrate to prevail on their motion to dismiss for improper venue? Even if venue is improper, the court may transfer to the case to a proper venue. Given that fact, what difference does it make whether venue was proper in the place where the plaintiff filed her action?

Unlike personal jurisdiction, where most of the analysis focuses on whether the assertion of jurisdiction violates the Due Process Clause, venue questions are a matter of statutory construction. Congress has created some specialized venue statutes for distinct forms of action, like statutory interpleader actions. But most venue questions are resolved under § 1391. Until 2011, § 1391 was divided into two subsections: § 1391(a) defined the proper venue for actions based solely on diversity, while § 1391(b) applied to actions not based solely on diversity. Finally, and sensibly, Congress amended § 1391.

As amended, § 1391(a) states that "this section shall govern the venue of all civil actions brought in the district courts of the United States." Section 1391(b) largely tracks the language of pre-2011 § 1391(a). Venue is proper in a district where all of the defendants reside, where a substantial part of the events took place, or if no other venue is proper, where the defendant is subject to personal jurisdiction. Prior to the amendments, the statute contained some ambiguity. For example, it provided that venue was proper where all defendants resided. Courts divided on the meaning of "resides" for individuals, with a majority construing that to mean the defendant's state of citizenship. The statute did not include a provision governing proper venue when the defendant was an unincorporated association. Courts treated unincorporated associations as if they were corporations. The statute did state that a corporation resided where it was subject to personal jurisdiction. Confused?

As amended in 2011, § 1391(c)(1) provides that "a natural person, including an alien lawfully admitted for permanent residence in the United States, shall be deemed to reside in the judicial district in which that person is domiciled." Further, § 1391(c)(2) equates an "entity with the capacity to sue or be sued in its common name under applicable law" to a corporation. That is, unincorporated organizations "reside" where they are subject to personal jurisdiction. One can question why Congress would treat venue as a matter of personal jurisdiction for some entities but as a matter of domicile for individuals. The advantage of the amendments, however, is that Congress has resolved the ambiguity in the previous version of the law.

Venue provisions are written in broad terms. Assuring access to a court is an important value within our system. Broadly drafted legislation assures that a plaintiff can find a proper venue; but it may also allow the plaintiff to choose a venue that is otherwise inconvenient.[2] As a result, in 1948, Congress enacted two statutes, giving federal courts power to transfer venue from one judicial district to another. Sections 1404 and 1406 contain some overlapping provisions: both allow transfer to another district "in the interests of justice" to another venue where the action could have been brought originally. But they are different in one significant way: § 1404 transfers are proper if the district where the action is pending is a proper venue;[3] § 1406 applies if the original venue is improper.

As a result, whether the original venue is proper or not, the court may transfer the venue. That begs a question: what difference does it make whether the original venue is proper? And here forum shopping surfaces again. In *Van Dusen v. Barrack,* 376 U.S. 612 (1964), plaintiffs, estate representatives of passengers who died in a plane crash in Boston, filed an action in a federal district court in Philadelphia, Pennsylvania. The defendant sought transfer to a federal district court in Boston, Massachusetts. Given the location of the accident, the motion to transfer seemed appropriate. Less obvious was the defendant's belief that upon transfer to Massachusetts, Massachusetts tort law (including a damages cap on wrongful death actions) would apply to the dispute. The Supreme Court held that Pennsylvania's choice of law would transfer along with the dispute (and presumably, under that law, Pennsylvania's law governing damages would apply).

More recently, a plaintiff, who lost part of his hand when he was working on a John Deere combine, failed to file his tort action within the statute of limitations in Pennsylvania where the accident occurred. His attorney filed the action in Mississippi, where, under Mississippi's choice of law rules, its longer statute of limitations applied to the action. Intent on conducting the trial closer to home, the plaintiff filed for a § 1404 transfer of venue back to Pennsylvania. The plaintiff needed the Court to extend *Van Dusen v. Barrack* to his situation, where the plaintiff made the transfer motion. The Supreme Court did just that in *Ferens v. John Deere Co.*, 494 U.S. 516 (1990).

*Van Dusen* and *Ferens* were premised on the fact that the original venue was proper. According to the Court, a change of venue properly chosen should not result in a change of law. The same cannot be said of a transfer pursuant to § 1406. As suggested in the brief description of *Van Dusen* and *Ferens,* whether the original district was a proper venue can have a profound effect on the litigation.

---

2. For some notable examples, take a look at *Piper Aircraft Co. v. Reyno,* 454 U.S. 235 (1981) and *Gulf Oil Corp. v. Gilbert,* 330 U.S. 501 (1947).

3. Section 1404 was also amended in 2011. Now, if the parties consent, the court may transfer the case to a district that would not have been a proper venue but for their consent.

# III. THE SIMULATION

As you saw in Chapter Two, once the Defendants have filed their motion challenging venue, the court has to decide how to proceed. As with personal jurisdiction, the parties may rely on affidavits; the court may order more detailed discovery, including depositions; or the court may conduct an evidentiary hearing.

Before reading further, consider whether the Central District of New York is a proper venue by examining § 1391. Consistent with F.R.C.P. 1 (the rules are designed "to secure the just, speedy, and inexpensive determination of every action and proceeding."), how should the parties and the court proceed with regard to the Defendants' venue challenge?

In moving to challenge venue, the Defendants would attach a memorandum of points and authorities on the venue question. The Plaintiff would counter with her own legal arguments. I have excluded those because the simulation requires you to make those arguments. Your professor has a number of options on how to proceed. For example, s/he may assign you a short writing assignment on the venue question or have you argue the motion orally in class or before someone serving as a magistrate judge. In addition to arguing whether venue is proper in the Central District of New York, be prepared to argue whether the court should transfer venue to a district in Connecticut. If so, should the court transfer under § 1404 or § 1406?

In analyzing whether the Central District of New York is a proper venue and whether the court should transfer the case to a district in Connecticut, consider the facts alleged in the complaint in Chapter Two. In addition to those facts, the Plaintiff has filed the following affidavit:

In the United States District Court

for the

Central District of New York

| | | |
|---|---|---|
| Sarah D. Nobile | ) | |
| Plaintiff | ) | Civil Action No. 00–123 |
| v. | ) | |
| Michael Ridge; and | ) | |
| MDC, Inc. | ) | |
| Defendants | ) | |

**DECLARATION OF SARAH D. NOBILE IN OPPOSITION TO DEFENDANTS' MOTION TO DISMISS FOR IMPROPER VENUE**

I, Sarah D. Nobile, file this declaration in opposition to the Defendants' Motion to Dismiss for Improper Venue.

1. I am the Plaintiff in the above-captioned action against Michael Ridge and MDC, Inc. Defendant Ridge is threatening to publish a false and

defamatory story in which he claims falsely that I possessed child pornography on my office computer when I worked for Connecticut State Appellate Judge John Elliot.

2. In YR-05, I graduated with high honors from Connecticut State University Law School. I was honored to receive an offer to serve as a law clerk to then-appellate Judge John Elliot. I happily accepted the job offer.

3. On June 1, YR-03, after serving as one of Judge Elliot's law clerk for almost two years, I was shocked when police, armed with a search warrant, raided Judge Elliot's chambers and seized two computers from the office.

4. I was even more shocked when I learned that police found child pornography on those computers and suspected me and the Judge of having down-loaded the offending files.

5. I was relieved to learn that Doddville District Attorney Clara Saint-Jean decided that the state had no case against me and the Judge. I was also relieved when I learned that she had agreed to order the search warrant sealed.

6. This experience made me fear that someone was trying to harm my reputation. As a result, I decided to seek employment in a state other than Connecticut. In YR-03, I accepted an offer of employment with the law firm of Breeze and Associates, LLC, with its main office in Cuomo City, New York.

7. In August, YR-03, I moved to Cuomo City to begin work for Breeze and Associates, LLC.

8. In August, YR-00, I received a phone call from Ms. Rhoda Sheen, the Judge's former secretary. She told me that she received a phone call from the Defendant Ridge, threatening to publish a story about the Judge and me. The story is to focus on the claim that we had child pornography on our computers and that, through his political connections, the Judge was able improperly to prevent our prosecutions.

9. I called Defendant Ridge and told him that these allegations are false and misleading. Unable to convince him not to publish the story, I began these proceedings.

10. On August 6, YR-00, I filed this action, including a motion for a temporary restraining order. On August 7, YR-00, this Court granted that motion. Thereafter, this Court granted a preliminary injunction preventing the Defendants from publishing the story.

11. Publication of the story will have a devastating effect on my life. I never downloaded child pornography. I have never looked at child pornography. I have never authorized anyone to download pornography on my computer. A story stating that I downloaded pornography on my computer would be defamatory. It would destroy my reputation and harm me irreparably. It would cause me even more emotional damage than I have already experienced.

12. Alternatively, a story stating that child pornography was found on my computer would be a violation of my privacy because it would imply that

I was responsible for pornography being on my computer. Even if technically true, such statements would put me in a false light. It would destroy my reputation and harm me irreparably. It would cause me even more emotional damage than I have already experienced.

I declare under penalty of perjury that the foregoing is true and correct.

Executed on this 26rd day of September, YR-00:

*Sarah D. Nobile*

Sarah D. Nobile

# IV. RELEVANT CASE LAW

Your casebook includes cases relevant to the interpretation of § 1391, § 1404, and § 1406. This section introduces you to some additional relevant case law.

Chapter One introduced you to the relevant tort law in New York and Connecticut. You saw that New York defamation law makes it more difficult for a plaintiff to prevail even in cases not involving public figures than does Connecticut law. New York law governing invasion of privacy is far more begrudging than is Connecticut law governing privacy claims. In discussing the decision where to file, you may have assumed that New York tort law would apply in New York courts, Connecticut tort law in Connecticut. This simulation is designed, in part, to get you to see why that may not be so.

In addition, even on the assumption that the court is going to transfer the case to a district in Connecticut, this simulation helps you to understand why the litigants care whether the transfer is based on § 1404 or § 1406. When more than one state may have an interest in the case before the court, a federal court, sitting in diversity, must apply the choice of law rules of the state in which it sits. The exception to that rule is when another court has transferred the case from another venue under § 1404. In that case, the transferee court applies the choice of law rules of the transferor court. Thus, in this case, if the Central District of New York is a proper venue, New York choice of law will travel with the case upon transfer to Connecticut.

As a result, you may need to know the choice of law rules in New York. Here is an excerpted discussion from a representative case from New York:

## PADULA v. LILARN PROPERTIES CORPORATION

644 N.E.2d 1001 (NY Ct. App.1994)

### OPINION OF THE COURT

SMITH, JUDGE.

Plaintiff is a resident of New York and defendant is a corporation incorporated under the laws of New York. Defendant owns property in Massachusetts, at which plaintiff was working, under a subcontracting agreement. Plaintiff sustained injuries when he fell from a scaffold while performing work on a construction project in Massachusetts. Plaintiff brought this action for damages, alleging violations of sections 200, 240(1) and 241(6) of the New York Labor Law and the rules and regulations thereunder. The issue here is the applicability of these sections of the Labor Law to this accident.

Defendant's motion for partial summary judgment dismissing plaintiff's causes of action alleging violations of the New York State Labor Law and various rules and regulations thereunder was granted by Supreme Court and affirmed by the Appellate Division, 198 A.D.2d 916, 604 N.Y.S.2d 464. Supreme Court thereafter granted defendant's motion for summary judgment dismissing the remainder of plaintiff's complaint. This Court granted leave from the Supreme Court judgment to bring up for review the prior nonfinal Appellate Division order (CPLR 5602[a][1][ii]).

We reject plaintiff's contention that New York law should apply here. New York's choice-of-law principles govern the outcome of this matter. In the context of tort law, New York utilizes interest analysis to determine which of two competing jurisdictions has the greater interest in having its law applied in the litigation. The greater interest is determined by an evaluation of the " 'facts or contacts which * * * relate to the purpose of the particular law in conflict' " * * *. Two separate inquiries are thereby required to determine the greater interest: (1) what are the significant contacts and in which jurisdiction are they located; and, (2) whether the purpose of the law is to regulate conduct or allocate loss. * * *

As to the first inquiry concerning the significant contacts and the jurisdiction in which they are located, both the plaintiff employee and the defendant owner of the Massachusetts property are domiciliaries of New York State. The other relevant actors are not parties to this lawsuit. They include the plaintiff's employer (a subcontractor which is a New York domiciliary), the tenant of the property (a Massachusetts domiciliary who contracted with the general contractor), and the general contractor (a domiciliary of Vermont). The tort occurred in Massachusetts.

As to the second inquiry, a distinction must be made between a choice-of-law analysis involving standards of conduct and one involving the allocation of losses * * * In the former case the law of the place of the tort governs. As we stated in *Schultz:*

> "Thus, when the conflicting rules involve the appropriate standards of conduct, rules of the road, for example, the law of the place of the tort 'will usually have a predominant, if not exclusive, concern' * * * because the locus jurisdiction's interests in protecting the reasonable expectations of the parties who relied on it to govern their primary conduct and in the admonitory effect that applying its law will have on similar conduct in the future assume critical importance and outweigh any interests of the common-domicile jurisdiction." * * *

Conduct-regulating rules have the prophylactic effect of governing conduct to prevent injuries from occurring. "If conflicting conduct-regulating laws are at issue, the law of the jurisdiction where the tort occurred will generally apply because that jurisdiction has the greatest interest in regulating behavior within its borders."

Loss allocating rules, on the other hand, are those which prohibit, assign, or limit liability after the tort occurs, such as charitable immunity statutes * * * wrongful death statutes * * * vicarious liability statutes * * * and contribution rules * * * Where the conflicting rules at issue are loss allocating and the parties to the lawsuit share a common domicile, the loss allocation rule of the common domicile will apply * * *.

Thus, the fundamental question in this case, where the parties share a common domicile, is whether Labor Law §§ 240 and 241 are primarily conduct-regulating or loss-allocating. The relevant Labor Law provisions, sections 240 and 241, embody both conduct-regulating and loss-allocating functions requiring worksites be made safe (conduct-regulating) and failure to do so results in strict and vicarious liability of the owner of the property or the general contractor. We hold however, that sections 240 and 241 of the Labor Law are primarily conduct-regulating rules, requiring that adequate safety measures be instituted at the worksite and should not be applied to the resolution of this tort dispute arising in Massachusetts. Thus, Massachusetts law was properly applied.

Accordingly, the judgment of Supreme Court appealed from and the order of the Appellate Division brought up for review should be affirmed, with costs.

# CHAPTER SIX

# MOTION TO DISMISS FOR FAILURE TO STATE A CLAIM FOR RELIEF

## I. INTRODUCTION

Chapter Two discussed briefly the options available to a defendant upon receiving a summons and complaint. After a brief discussion of procedural systems other than the F.R.C.P., this chapter consists of the Plaintiff's complaint, some questions that counsel for the Defendants should consider in deciding how to proceed, and an assignment for this simulation, including relevant case law.

## II. PLEADING AND MOTIONS: SOME BACKGROUND

When I was a young lawyer, a senior lawyer made a comment to me that did not resonate until I began teaching Civil Procedure. He stated that most lawyers do not appreciate the philosophy evident in the F.R.C.P. or, for that matter, in any procedural system.

Probably most students expect their Civil Procedure course to be about dull stuff, like the number of days in which to file an answer after receiving the complaint. And even when they begin the course, most probably fail to see the important policy choices woven into a procedural code. Recognizing those policies both enlivens a course on procedure and improves a student's understanding of procedure.

Rules governing pleading demonstrate the point quite well. Civil litigation in the United States has been dominated by three pleading systems.

The first important system was common law pleading. Although largely abandoned today, it has left its mark on modern pleading. Its arcane rules help to explain the goals of modern systems. A plaintiff seeking to sue in a common law pleading system needed to select the right writ for the type of case the plaintiff hoped to bring to court. Further, common law systems did not allow discovery. Instead, litigants developed facts and narrowed issues through a series of pleadings that were supposed to lead the parties to the facts in issue, which could then be resolved at trial.

In torts, a plaintiff might bring an action on the writ of trespass to recover damages for battery. But if at trial, she proved the defendant acted negligently, the plaintiff lost her case because her proof varied from the writ that she brought. The system was arcane and formalistic, turning on skillful lawyering rather than on whether the defendant had harmed the plaintiff in violation of the plaintiff's rights.

Reform occurred by the mid–1800s with the wide adoption of Code pleading. New York adopted the Field Code in 1848. Named after David Dudley Field, the Code dominated state pleading for many years and remains in place in many states. It abandoned the writ system, limited the rounds of pleading, and put in place rules allowing some discovery.

Most Civil Procedure casebooks introduce students to some of the failings of Code pleading. Code pleading requires a plaintiff to state facts sufficient to demonstrate that she has a cause of action. Many state courts have developed hyper-technical interpretations of those terms. A plaintiff is not supposed to plead legal conclusions or evidence, but instead is supposed to plead material, essential and ultimate facts upon which the plaintiff's right of action is based. Editors of casebooks have an easy time finding cases from different states but involving similar allegations that come to opposite conclusions whether the pleading is sufficient.

Whether such distinctions matter depend on other questions. For example, what is the penalty for failing to plead correctly? Does the system allow liberal amendment or is the improper pleading fatal to the plaintiff's case? Also, what interests are served by the distinctions developed by state courts? Is the defendant prejudiced by a plaintiff's imprecise pleading? If not, then a dismissal on the merits is a bonanza for the defendant, allowing the defendant to get away with harming the plaintiff without having to answer in court. Consider too whether as a general matter plaintiffs or defendants can hire skilled attorneys able to negotiate complex rules. If a society favors access to its court system to allow injured parties to redress grievances, decisions making successful pleading difficult harm less affluent plaintiffs.

The history leading to the passage of the Rules Enabling Act (giving the Court the responsibility to create rules of practice and procedure) is fascinating, but largely beyond the scope of this book and Civil Procedure casebooks.[1] But you can see progressive influences in the pleading rules adopted by the Court and Congress in the F.R.C.P. Rejecting the arcane distinctions that developed in Code pleading states, the drafters of the F.R.C.P. provided that a complaint must contain "a short plain statement of the claim showing that the pleader is entitled to relief." See F.R.C.P. 8(a)(2). The rules also provide model forms. An examination of the rule, its history, and the sample forms underscore that the drafters wanted to get courts out of the business of dismissing cases on the pleading in most cases.

Two examples underscore the differences between Code and federal pleading. In Code pleading systems, a plaintiff who stated that his suit was

1. For those interested in additional reading, I recommend Edward A. Purcell, Jr., *Brandeis and the Progressive Constitution* (2000), which provides not only an excellent history of the politics behind the passage of the R.E.A. but also a remarkable study of *Erie Railroad Co. v. Tompkins,* 304 U.S. 64 (1938).

based on the defendant's negligence most likely plead improperly. Courts in Code pleading states often characterize an allegation of "negligence" as improper because it is a legal conclusion. Some courts came to a contrary conclusion. But one should ask what is at stake if a plaintiff pleads that the defendant engaged in negligent conduct. Is the defendant aware of what she is being called into court for? If so, what is accomplished by dismissing the complaint or forcing the plaintiff to re-plead her case? The relevant form in the F.R.C.P made clear that a complaint stating that the defendant acted negligently was not objectionable.[2] The goal of the complaint, according to the drafters of Rule 8, is to give the defendant adequate notice of what he is being called into court for. If the pleading is insufficient, the rules allow the defendant to move for a more definite statement.

The other example is *Dioguardi v. Durning,* 139 F.2d 774 (2nd Cir. 1944), written by Judge Charles Clark, one of the primary drafters of the F.R.C.P. Dioguardi was a barely literate pro se litigant whose complaint alleged improper conduct by the Collector of Customs in New York.[3] The lower court granted the defendant's motion to dismiss the complaint for failure to state a claim for relief under F.R.C.P. 12(b)(6) after initially allowing Dioguardi to amend his complaint. The lower court did so because the complaint "fails to state facts sufficient to constitute a cause of action." No doubt an embarrassing moment for the trial court, Judge Clark observed that the new rules (in force since 1938) contained no such requirement.

Judge Clark's opinion demonstrates the philosophy behind the rules. Instead of reading the complaint technically against the drafter of the complaint, he observed that the court should take as true the allegations in the complaint and all reasonable inference from those facts. A trial court should dismiss the complaint only if, when viewed in a light most favorable to the pleader, the complaint failed to state a claim for relief.

After reading *Dioguardi,* students understand the choices that the drafters made: injured parties can gain access to court without meeting technical objections. Thereafter, the parties proceed to discovery. Thus, the rules favor lay people or lawyers not versed in highly technical rules. Dismissal on the pleading should be rare. As you will see later, the rules contemplate that cases lacking merit should be dismissed after discovery, upon summary judgment. But that should occur only if discovery does not demonstrate genuine factual disputes.

Any procedural system invites abuse. During the 1970s and 1980s, lower courts experienced a sharp increase in their dockets. The defense bar argued that the increase resulted, in part, from liberal pleading rules and those rules led to the filing of frivolous lawsuits.[4] During the 1980s, discovery rules and Rule 11 were amended to address these concerns. But the drafters of the rules did not amend F.R.C.P. 8.

2. See, e.g., Form 11 Complaint for Negligence in the F.R.C.P. ("On [Date], at [Place], the defendant negligently drove a motor vehicle against the plaintiff.")

3. The plaintiff may have been Johnny Dioguardi, a New York mobster. A former student brought that to my attention but further research efforts have not confirmed or rebutted that fact. The mobster was living in New York around the time of the suit.

4. The accuracy of those claims has been hotly disputed.

Despite that, some lower courts developed heightened pleading standards in some classes of cases. For example, because some courts believed that plaintiffs in civil rights were more likely to file frivolous lawsuits than in other categories of cases, those courts developed "common law" requirements of more particularized pleading in such cases. The Supreme Court repeatedly rejected those efforts. After all, the rules provide in narrow instances for heightened pleading. See F.R.C.P. 9.

That trend ended in 2007 and continued in 2009. In 2007, the Court decided *Bell Atlantic Corp. v. Twombly,* 550 U.S. 544 (2007), holding that the plaintiffs' class action complaint failed to state a claim for relief. Early reaction to *Twombly* was relatively mild; many observers thought that the case was limited to antitrust cases. That proved untrue when the Court decided *Ashcroft v. Iqbal,* 556 U.S. 662 (2009), which explicitly rejected the narrow reading of *Twombly.*

This simulation requires you to explore those two cases. I offer a word of caution as you begin working on this simulation and reading those cases. Lower courts are deeply divided over the meaning of those two decisions. An overly broad reading of the cases guts the liberal pleading policies in place for over 70 years. Such a broad reading of those cases also may make a plaintiff's lawsuit impossible, even though she may have a meritorious claim: if she fails at the pleading stage, she cannot get to discovery. Without discovery, she may be unable to prove her case. Further, the opinions contain language that seesaws back and forth between narrow and broad interpretations of F.R.C.P. 12(b)(6).

In considering this exercise, remember the dilemma facing the Plaintiff. She has an obligation to conduct a reasonable investigation before filing her suit. But courts consider the exigencies when determining whether a plaintiff conducted a "reasonable investigation." As discussed in other chapters, Ms. Nobile must file her suit quickly and without putting the Defendant's on notice that she is going to sue. Consider what would happen to her case if she has to plead too specifically at this early stage of the proceeding.

For purposes of this exercise, you will see that Ms. Nobile has filed her action in federal court in Connecticut, based on her claim that some of the Defendants violated her rights under § 1983 and that others conspired to do so.

## III. THE LAWSUIT: THE COMPLAINT[5]

In the United States District Court

for the

District of Connecticut

| | | |
|---|---|---|
| Sarah D. Nobile,<br>Plaintiff<br>v.<br>Department of Police for<br>The City of Doddville;<br>MDC, Inc.; Nathan Loewe;<br>Michael Ridge; and<br>Unnamed Officers of<br>The DPCCD;<br>Defendants | )<br>)<br>)<br>)<br>)<br>)<br>)<br>)<br>)<br>) | No. 00–34–1689 |

### COMPLAINT

Plaintiff Sarah D. Nobile, on personal knowledge as to her own acts, and on information and belief as to all others based on its investigation, alleges as follows:

### NATURE OF THE ACTION

1. Plaintiff, Sarah D. Nobile, brings this action against the above-captioned defendants for violating her constitutional right to be free from an unreasonable search; for conspiring to violate her constitutional right to be free from an unreasonable search; for violating her right to privacy; and for conspiring to violate her right to privacy.

### STATEMENT OF JURISDICTION

2. This case arises under 28 U.S.C. § 1983. State law claims are within the Court's supplemental jurisdiction under 28 U.S.C. § 1367(a). In addition, the Plaintiff is a citizen of New York and the Defendants are all citizens of Connecticut and the amount in controversy, without interests and costs, exceeds the sum value specified by 28 U.S.C. § 1332.

### FACTUAL BACKGROUND

3. On August 28, YR-05, Plaintiff began working for Connecticut State Judge John Elliot.

4. During her period of employment for Judge Elliot, Plaintiff worked in Judge Elliot's Chambers in the Appellate Court Building, 123 Nutley Avenue, Hartford, Connecticut.

---

5. Along with this complaint, the Plaintiff filed a motion for a temporary restraining order, which the court granted.

5. As part of her job, Plaintiff was assigned a workstation in an office shared with Judge Elliot's other law clerk, Defendant Nathan Loewe.

6. Plaintiff's workstation included a Dell Computer, with access to the Internet, which she was allowed to use to conduct legal research on various legal data bases.

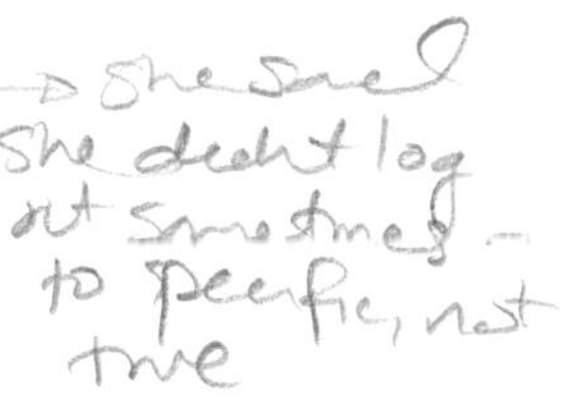

7. At all times, Plaintiff followed office policy and used her computer for proper business purposes only.

8. On June 1, YR-03, Defendants unnamed members of Doddville City Police Department executed a search warrant for Judge Elliot's chambers.

9. During the course of the search, a member of the Police Department removed two computers from Judge Elliot's chambers.

10. On June 10, YR-03, a technician working for the Defendant Police Department, allegedly found child pornography on two of the computers, including Plaintiff's.

11. Because of serious questions about the legality of the warrant and because many other people had access to the computers, the Doddville District Attorney's Office refused to prosecute Plaintiff.

12. For reasons stated in Paragraph 10, the Doddville District Attorney Clara Saint-Jean agreed to seal the warrant because of concerns that revealing information about the search would unfairly damage Plaintiff's and others' reputations.

13. At some time prior to August 3, YR-00, one or more of the individual Defendants (Nathan Loewe or one of the unnamed police officers) leaked information about the contents of the sealed search warrant to Defendant Michael Ridge.

14. On August 3, YR-00, Plaintiff received a phone call from Judge Elliot's former secretary, Rhoda Sheen, who told her that Defendant Michael Ridge was threatening to publish an article claiming that Plaintiff and Judge Elliot were guilty of possessing child pornography on their office computers.

15. Also on August 3, YR-00, with the hope of stopping the publication of a false and defamatory story, Plaintiff called Defendant Ridge and left a voicemail in which she told him of her concerns.

16. Defendant Ridge called Plaintiff on August 4, YR-00 and told her that he was going to name her in the story and post it on his Web site GOTCHA! He also told her that the main focus of the story was Judge Elliot, whom Defendant Ridge called a hypocrite, and intimated that if Plaintiff would be a source confirming the facts in the story about the Judge, he would delete her name.

17. Plaintiff begged for time to consider what to do. She brings this suit to stop publication of a false and defamatory article that may go "viral" on the Internet, permanently harming her reputation.

### COUNT ONE

18. Paragraphs 3-17 are hereby incorporated by reference. Defendants Unnamed Officers violated the Plaintiff's Fourth Amendment right to be free from an unreasonable search. Their conduct violated the Plaintiff's rights protected by 42 U.S.C. § 1983.

### COUNT TWO

19. Paragraphs 3-17 are hereby incorporated by reference. Defendants Unnamed Officers and Defendant Nathan Loewe conspired to violate the Plaintiff's Fourth Amendment right to be free from an unreasonable search. Their conduct violated the Plaintiff's rights protected by 42 U.S.C. § 1983.

### COUNT THREE

20. Paragraphs 3-17 are hereby incorporated by reference. Defendant Ridge plans to publish a story alleging that Plaintiff possessed child pornography. That publication violates her right to privacy. Specifically, even a statement limited to the fact that child pornography was found on her computer puts Plaintiff in a false light.

### COUNT FOUR

21. Paragraphs 3-17 are hereby incorporated by reference. Defendants Unnamed Officers, Defendant Nathan Loewe, and Defendant Michael Ridge are liable to Plaintiff for violating her rights of privacy protected by Connecticut law. That conspiracy resulted in Defendant Ridge learning of private information discovered through the illegal search of her computer.

### COUNT FIVE

22. Paragraphs 3-17 are hereby incorporated by reference. Defendant MDC, Inc. is liable to Plaintiff under the theory of respondeat superior as Defendant Ridge's employer.

### COUNT SIX

23. Paragraphs 3-17 are hereby incorporated by reference. Defendant Department of Police for the City of Doddville is liable to Plaintiff under the theory of respondeat superior as Defendant Unnamed Officers' employer.

### PRAYER FOR RELIEF

24. Plaintiff requests that this Court enjoin all of the Defendants and all persons acting in concert with Defendants from publishing or otherwise disseminating any information concerning allegations child pornography was found on Plaintiff's computer or in any other way linking her to illegal activity based on the search of Judge Elliot's chambers.

25. Plaintiff requests damages in such amount as the court shall determine to compensate Plaintiff for her damages suffered as a result of Defendants conduct.

26. Plaintiff requests punitive damages in such amount as the court shall determine to punish Defendants for their outrageous and unlawful conduct.

27. Plaintiff requests her costs of suit and reasonable attorneys' fees;

28. Plaintiff requests such other relief to which she may be entitled.

Respectfully submitted,

*Adrian Connell*

Adrian Connell
139 McGeorge Avenue
Cuomo City, New York 11774
(561) 782–1897

Dated: September 30, YR-00

## IV. THE DEFENDANTS' STRATEGY

Consider the various challenges that you have studied up to this point. Because Ms. Nobile's attorney filed suit in Connecticut, counsel for the Defendants are not be able to object to personal jurisdiction. Examine 28 U.S.C. § 1391 and consider why they would not be able to make a successful venue challenge. For purposes of this simulation, assume that the court has subject matter jurisdiction based on 28 U.S.C. § 1331, in conjunction with § 1367(a).

Focus now on other options available to the Defendants. Examine Federal Rules 7, 8 and 12(a) and 12(b) and consider the best option at this stage in the proceedings. What would the best outcome be for the Defendants at this early stage of the proceedings?

## V. THE SIMULATION EXERCISE

This simulation consists of two parts.

(A) Assume that you work for the firm that represents Michael Ridge and Nathan Loewe.[6] The partner explains that s/he is still considering whether to file an answer and including a Rule 12(b)(6) challenge to the complaint or whether to file a pre-answer Rule 12(b)(6) challenge. In either case, s/he needs to get some information from Mr. Ridge and Mr. Loewe and has told you to prepare questions for the meeting with the two men.

(B) After consulting with Mr. Ridge and Mr. Loewe, the senior partner prepared the following joint motion to dismiss. Consistent with F.R.C.P. 11, s/he wants to be sure that the motion has merit and asks you for your thoughts. Your professor may have you present your thoughts orally or to

6. Assume that counsel can do this without a conflict of interest.

submit a short memorandum explaining whether the following motion to dismiss has merit. In responding to your senior partner, review the New York invasion of privacy case *Freihofer v. Hearst, Corp.* and the Connecticut invasion of privacy case *Goodrich v. Waterbury Republican–American, Inc.,* which you will find in Chapter Two. In addition, s/he asks you to consider *O'Connor v. O'Connor*, which you will find below. As you will see when you read the Motion to Dismiss, the court will have to consider Connecticut choice of law rules in deciding one of Defendant Ridge's contentions.

In the United States District Court

for the

District of Connecticut

| | | |
|---|---|---|
| Sarah D. Nobile, | ) | |
| Plaintiff | ) | No. 00–34–1689 |
| v. | ) | |
| Department of Police for | ) | |
| The City of Doddville; | ) | |
| MDC, Inc.; Nathan Loewe; | ) | |
| Michael Ridge; and | ) | |
| Unnamed Officers of | ) | |
| The DPCCD; | ) | |
| Defendants | ) | |

**JOINT MOTION TO DISMISS FOR FAILURE TO STATE A CLAIM FOR RELIEF**

Pursuant to Rule 12(b)(6), Defendants Michael Ridge and Nathan Loewe move the Court to dismiss Counts Two, Three and Four of the Plaintiff's Complaint with prejudice.

As developed more fully in the attached **Memorandum of Points and Authorities in Support of Defendants Michael Ridge and Nathan Loewe's Joint Motion to Dismiss for Failure to State a Claim for Relief:**

1. With regard to Count Two and Four, under recent Supreme Court precedent, a plaintiff must allege more than a mere conspiracy between various defendants to satisfy F.R.C.P. 8(a)(2) and F.R.C.P. 12(b)(6).

2. With regard to Count Three and Four, this Court must apply Connecticut's choice of law principles. Under Connecticut choice of law, this Court must apply New York tort law and under New York tort law, the Plaintiff has no claim for relief for an invasion of privacy.

Wherefore, Defendants Michael Ridge and Nathan Loewe ask this Court to dismiss Counts Two, Three and Four for failure to state a claim for relief.

Respectfully submitted,

*R. Cooper Russell*

R. Cooper Russell
Russell and Scott
Attorneys at Law
Suite 6
McGeorge Towers
Cuomo City, New York 11774
(561) 782–0099

Attorney for Defendants Michael Ridge
and Nathan Loewe

Dated: October 12, YR-00

**CERTIFICATE OF SERVICE**

I hereby certify that on August 26, YR-00, I caused the following document:

DEFENDANT RIDGE'S MOTION TO DISMISS UNDER RULE 12(b)(6) FOR FAILURE TO STATE A CLAIM FOR RELIEF

to be served on the plaintiff and plaintiff's counsel, Adrian Connell, by first class mail, postage paid.

Dated: October 12, YR-00

Respectfully submitted,

*R. Cooper Russell*

R. Cooper Russell
Russell and Scott
Attorneys at Law
Suite 6
McGeorge Towers
Cuomo City, New York 11774
(561) 782–0099

Attorney for Defendants Michael Ridge and
Nathan Loewe

# VI. CONNECTICUT CHOICE OF LAW

In Chapters One and Five, you have seen the importance of choice of law rules. Here again, you can see its importance for deciding whether someone gets her day in court and how one of the parties raises the issue. Here is a thoughtful decision by the Connecticut Supreme Court, applicable to deciding the motion above.

## O'CONNOR v. O'CONNOR

519 A.2d 13 (Conn. 1986)

PETERS, CHIEF JUSTICE.

The sole issue on this appeal is whether, under the circumstances of this case, an injured person may pursue a cause of action under Connecticut law to recover for allegedly tortious conduct that occurred in a jurisdiction where such a cause of action would not be permitted. The plaintiff, Roseann O'Connor, brought an action against the defendant, Brian O'Connor, seeking damages for injuries that she suffered as a result of an automobile accident in Quebec.[1] The trial court, *Reilly, J.*, granted the defendant's motion to strike the complaint, finding that the law of Quebec, the place of injury, governed the controversy and that Quebec law precluded the plaintiff's action. Thereafter, the court, *S. Freedman, J.*, rendered a judgment in favor of the defendant. The plaintiff appealed to the Appellate Court, which, in a per curiam opinion, upheld the trial court's judgment. We reverse the judgment of the Appellate Court.

The relevant facts are undisputed. The plaintiff was injured as a result of a one car automobile accident that occurred on September 3, 1981, in the province of Quebec, Canada. At the time of the accident, the defendant was operating the automobile and the plaintiff was his sole passenger. The parties, both of whom were Connecticut domiciliaries, were on a one day pleasure trip that began, and was intended to end, in Vermont. The plaintiff underwent hospital treatment for her injuries in Quebec and has suffered continuing physical disabilities while residing in Connecticut.

The plaintiff brought an action against the defendant on August 17, 1983, alleging that she had suffered serious and permanent injuries as a result of the defendant's negligent operation of the automobile. The plaintiff's complaint stated a cause of action permitted by General Statutes § 38–323, * * * part of Connecticut's No-fault Motor Vehicle Insurance Act, General Statutes §§ 38–319 through 38–350. Section 38–323 permits the victim of serious physical or economic injury caused by an automobile accident to sue the tortfeasor for damages. The defendant, however, moved to strike the complaint, on the ground that the applicable law in the case was the law of Quebec. Quebec law would not permit the plaintiff's tort action because Quebec Revised Statutes, chapter A–25, title II, §§ 3 and 4, provides instead for government

1. The parties were not related at the time of the accident. They subsequently married each other.

funded compensation for victims of bodily injury caused by automobile accidents. * * *

After a hearing, the trial court, *Reilly, J.,* granted the motion to strike in an oral decision. The court expressly based its decision on this court's opinion in *Gibson v. Fullin,* 172 Conn. 407, 374 A.2d 1061 (1977), our most recent decision affirming the doctrine that the nature and extent of tort liability is governed by the place of injury, hereinafter referred to as "lex loci delicti" or "lex loci." When judgment was subsequently rendered in favor of the defendant, the plaintiff appealed to the Appellate Court, which, like the trial court, considered itself bound by this court's past adherence to the lex loci doctrine. Accordingly, the Appellate Court, in a per curiam opinion, affirmed the judgment of the trial court. * * *

On appeal to this court, the plaintiff argues that the trial court erred in granting the defendant's motion to strike. Recognizing that the trial court and the Appellate Court accurately applied the rules governing conflict of laws that our Connecticut cases have previously articulated, the plaintiff urges this court to reexamine the propriety of our continued adherence to the doctrine of lex loci delicti in cases of personal injury. In the particular circumstances of this case, the plaintiff maintains, we should no longer adhere rigidly to the doctrine of lex loci but should instead seek to discern and to apply the law of the jurisdiction that has the most significant relationship to the controversy, in accordance with the principles of the Restatement Second of Conflict of Laws. Under the Restatement, according to the plaintiff, the jurisdiction that has the most significant relationship to this tort action is not Quebec but Connecticut. Quebec, although it was the place of injury, has no significant interest in applying its statutory compensation scheme to the controversy because the location of the automobile accident in Quebec was purely fortuitous. Connecticut, by contrast, has a substantial interest in applying its law to the case because: (1) both parties are domiciled and employed in Connecticut; (2) both parties are subject to the requirements and entitled to the benefits of Connecticut's no-fault insurance law, and that law embodies a policy of providing access to the courts for persons with serious bodily injuries; and (3) aside from her initial treatment after the accident, the plaintiff has received all of her postaccident medical care in Connecticut. We agree with the plaintiff.

I

This court has traditionally adhered to the doctrine that the substantive rights and obligations arising out of a tort controversy are determined by the law of the place of injury, or lex loci delicti. * * * Recently, however, we have recognized that there are circumstances in which strict application of the lex loci delicti rule frustrates the legitimate expectations of the parties and undermines an important policy of this state. In such circumstances, we have refused to apply the doctrine. * * * *Simaitis* was a plaintiff's appeal of an adverse summary judgment in a negligence action arising out of an automobile accident that occurred in Tennessee. The parties were Connecticut domiciliaries employed by a Connecticut corporation. The accident occurred while they were traveling in the course of their employment. The dispositive issue on appeal was whether the governing law was the workers' compensation act of Tennessee, which barred the plaintiff's action for damages, or the Connecticut act, which permitted such an action. We held that application of the lex loci rule in these circumstances afforded an "unsatisfactory resolution" to the choice of law problem; * * * noting that to employ the rule "would bestow upon temporary visitors injured in Connecticut all the relief which the Connecticut compensation act affords, but deny that same relief to Connecticut residents injured while on temporary business outside the state, even when all other incidents of employment ... are in Connecticut." * * * Although we expressly declined to reconsider the rule of lex loci for tort law in general, we decided that it was appropriate to pursue an alternate approach for choice of law issues in workers' compensation cases. The alternate approach that we adopted looked to an examination of the respective interests of the relevant jurisdictions in applying their law to the controversy, and turned for guidance to the principles of § 181 of the Restatement Second of Conflict of Laws. * * * Applying the principles of the Restatement, we held that the law of Connecticut, and not that of Tennessee, should govern the plaintiff's right to recover. * * *

Our decision in *Simaitis* has rightly been interpreted as a signal that we are not wholeheartedly committed to application of lex loci as the sole approach to choice of law in all torts cases. * * * Similarly, two federal district court cases have interpreted dicta in *Gibson v. Fullin,* supra, as contemplating circumstances in which Connecticut courts might deviate from the lex loci doctrine provided a "compelling reason" exists to do so. * * *

II

We have consistently held that "a court should not overrule its earlier decisions unless the most cogent reasons and inescapable logic requires it." * * * We have also recognized, however, that "[p]rinciples of law which serve one generation well may, by reason of changing conditions, disserve a later one," and that "[e]xperience can and often does demonstrate that a rule, once believed sound, needs modification to serve justice better." * * * Accordingly, we now undertake to analyze the policies and principles underlying the doctrine of lex loci delicti, as a preliminary step to determining whether "cogent reasons and inescapable logic" demand that we abandon the doctrine under the circumstances of the present case.

The doctrine of lex loci delicti, as first adopted by American courts in the late nineteenth and early twentieth century, presumes that the rights and obligations of the parties to a tort action "vest" at the place of injury. See 3 J. Beale, Conflict of Laws (1935) p. 1968. Justice Cardozo, describing the vested rights theory in *Loucks v. Standard Oil Co.,* 224 N.Y. 99, 110, 120 N.E. 198 (1918), stated: "A foreign statute is not law in this state, but it gives rise to an obligation, which, if transitory, 'follows the person and may be enforced wherever the person may be found.... [I]t is a principle of every civilized law that vested rights shall be protected' (Beale, [Conflict of Laws], § 51)." In one of the earliest Connecticut decisions to recognize the lex loci doctrine, this court held: "The right of action for the injury is inseparable from its extent, hence the measure of damages as well as the right of recovery are determined by the place of the injury.... Such an obligation, or right of action, as a general rule, becomes vested, and will be enforced here precisely as if the obligation or right of action had accrued or arisen in this jurisdiction." * * * The vested rights theory was a guiding principle of the first Restatement of Conflict of Laws. See Restatement, Conflict of Laws (1934) §§ 377 through 379.

The vested rights theory of choice of law is an anachronism in modern jurisprudence. Its underlying premise, that the legislative jurisdiction of the place where a right "vests" must be recognized in every other jurisdiction, presupposes that a nationally uniform system of choice of law rules is necessary and desirable. See R. Leflar, American Conflicts Law (1968) pp. 205–206. Choice of law rules are not immutable principles, however. Subject to the limitations of the due process clause of the fourteenth amendment * * * and the full faith and credit clause of article IV, § 1, of the United States constitution, * * *; individual state courts are free to formulate choice of law rules as they deem appropriate. "[F]or a State's substantive law to be selected in a constitutionally permissible manner, that State must have a significant contact or significant aggregation of contracts, creating state interests, such that choice of its law is neither arbitrary nor fundamentally unfair." * * *.

Stripped of the mantle of constitutional authority, the vested rights doctrine is simply another legal theory, and one which has been the subject of extensive criticism for the past half century. * * *. Professor David F. Cavers criticized the vested rights doctrine as ignoring the substantive content of legal rules and focusing exclusively on territorial concerns, "the law's content being irrelevant to the choice" of law. D. Cavers, Re–Stating the Conflict of Laws: The Chapter on Contracts, *in* XXth Century Comparative and Conflicts Law (1961) pp. 349, 350. Another, more fundamental criticism of the vested rights theory of conflicts of law is that it fails to explain "why the law of the place of wrong should be applied to cases which have arisen there. [It gives] us a guiding principle but without any *raison d'etre.*" N. Hancock, Torts in the Conflict of Laws (1942) p. 36.

The theoretical barrenness of the vested rights doctrine, from which the rule of lex loci delicti derives, is but one of the many reasons that a majority of state courts have rejected the rule of lex loci, and that legal scholars have virtually unanimously urged its abandonment. "The basic theme running through the attacks on the place of injury rule is that wooden application of a few overly simple rules, based on the outmoded 'vested rights theory,' cannot solve the complex problems which arise in modern litigation and may often yield harsh, unnecessary and unjust results." *Griffith v. United Air Lines, Inc.,* 416 Pa. 1, 13, 203 A.2d 796 (1964). The lex loci approach fails to acknowledge that jurisdictions other than the place of injury may have a legitimate interest in applying their laws to resolve particular issues arising out of a tort controversy. * * *

Having noted the perceived weaknesses of a categorical lex loci delicti rule, we now consider the principal reasons advanced for its retention. These are: (1) the desirability of allowing the legislature to alter established choice of law doctrines; (2) stare decisis; (3) the certainty and predictability of result afforded by a categorical choice of law rule and the concomitant ease of applying such a rule; and (4) the prevention of parochial applications of forum law in controversies involving foreign jurisdictions. * * * We will examine each of these rationales in turn as they relate to the circumstances of the present case.

Because choice of law is a matter of "broad public policy," the defendant argues that it is the province of the legislature, and not the courts, to make doctrinal changes in established law. Some of the courts that have chosen to adhere to the lex loci doctrine have expressed similar sentiments. * * * We disagree. The lex loci doctrine is the creation of jurists and scholars, not legislators. * * * Statutes deal expressly with choice of law issues only rarely and episodically. * * * The defendant's reliance, in this regard, on General Statutes § 52–572d is misplaced. That statute *abolishes* the rule of lex loci delicti in actions for injuries caused by motor vehicle accidents occurring in jurisdictions which recognize interspousal immunity. The fact that, in § 52–572d, the legislature overruled a line of our decisions holding that the availability of the interspousal immunity defense depends on the law of the place of injury; see, e.g., *Landers v. Landers,* 153 Conn. 303, 304, 216 A.2d 183 (1966); hardly advances the defendant's argument that the legislature has implicitly *approved* of the lex loci doctrine. The legislature of course retains plenary authority, subject to constitutional mandates, to formulate statutory choice of law rules. Until the legislature chooses to act, however, this court has an independent responsibility to modernize rules of law that have traditionally reposed with the judiciary.

Regarding stare decisis, the second argument in favor of retaining lex loci, we have already noted that, while courts should not overrule established precedent except in compelling circumstances, the force of precedent will not hinder our rejection of a rule whose application no longer serves the ends of justice. * * * The arguments for adherence to precedent are least compelling, furthermore, "when the rule to be discarded may not be reasonably supposed to have determined the conduct of the litigants, and particularly when in its origin it was the product of institutions or conditions which have gained a new significance or development with the progress of the years." * * * In the present case, as in most unintentional tort cases, there is no reason to suppose that the defendant planned his conduct with the intention of availing himself of the benefits of Quebec law. "Rarely do parties contemplate the consequences of tortious conduct, and rarely if at all will they give thought to the question of what law would be applied to govern their conduct if it were to result in injury." * * * Our refusal to adhere to lex loci delicti in this case, therefore, does not defeat any legitimate prelitigation expectations of the parties founded in reliance on our prior decisions. * * *

The third argument in favor of retention of the doctrine of lex loci is that it imparts certainty, predictability, and ease of application to choice of law rules. We do not underestimate these characteristics. "Simplicity in law is a virtue. Judicial efficiency often depends upon it." R. Leflar, "Choice–Influencing Considerations in Conflicts Law," 41 N.Y.U.L.Rev. 267, 288 (1966). The virtue of simplicity must, however, be balanced against the vice of arbitrary and inflexible application of a rigid rule. "Ease of determining applicable law and uniformity of rules of decision ... must be subordinated to the objective of proper choice of law in conflict cases, i.e., to determine the law that most appropriately applies to the issue involved...." * * * In the present case, application of the lex loci delicti doctrine makes determination of the governing law turn upon a purely fortuitous circumstance: the geographical location of the parties' automobile at the time the accident occurred. Choice of law must not be rendered a matter of happenstance, in which the respective interests of the parties and the concerned jurisdictions receive only coincidental consideration. Numerous jurisdictions have declined to apply the law of the place of injury in similar circumstances. * * *

We note, furthermore, that lex loci's arguable advantages of uniformity and predictability have been undermined by its widespread rejection by courts and scholars, and by judicial constructions that avoid its strict application. Lex loci "no longer affords even a semblance of the general application that was once thought to be its great virtue." * * * Even when it was the dominant American choice of law rule, courts frequently took advantage of various "escape devices" that allowed them to pay lip service to lex loci while avoiding its strict application. * * * Such devices included characterizing the issue at stake as procedural, rather than substantive, so that the law of the forum could be applied; * * * or characterizing a complaint framed in tort as a contract matter, thus allowing the law governing the place of contracting, rather than the place of injury, to control. * * * Because the use of such evasive devices undermines the predictability and ease of application of the lex loci doctrine, their use has been widely disparaged by scholarly commentators. "[I]t is a poor defense of the system to say that the unacceptable results which [lex loci] will inevitably produce can be averted by disingenuousness if the courts are sufficiently alert." * * *

We now consider the fourth principal argument in favor of retention of lex loci, that application of the doctrine prevents forum courts from exercising parochial favoritism. Without lex loci, there is a risk that the forum will not take seriously the foreign jurisdiction's legitimate interest in the controversy. * * * How seriously this risk is viewed depends upon an assessment of the available alternatives. "The alternative to a hard and fast system of doctrinal formulae is not anarchy. The difference is not between a system and no system, but between two systems; between a system which purports to have, but lacks, complete logical symmetry and one which affords latitude for the interplay and clash of conflicting factors." * * * Existing case law in other jurisdictions demonstrates that conflicts principles need not depend solely upon lex loci to assure proper deference to the legitimate claims of foreign law. A principled search for the local law of the state with the most significant relationship to the occurrence and the parties will often cause foreign law to be recognized as the law that should govern the controversy. * * * "There is no reason why [a judge] should be less dispassionate in a conflicts case than in any other." * * *

We are, therefore, persuaded that the time has come for the law in this state to abandon categorical allegiance to the doctrine of lex loci delicti in tort actions. Lex loci has lost its theoretical underpinnings. Its formerly broad base of support has suffered erosion. We need not decide today, however, whether to discard lex loci in all of its manifestations. It is sufficient for us to consider whether, in the circumstances of the present case, reason and justice require the relaxation of its stringent insistence on determining conflicts of laws solely by reference to the place where a tort occurred.

In deciding how to assess a replacement for lex loci, we recognize that the legal literature offers us various alternative approaches to the problems of choice of law. Three such approaches have gained widespread judicial acceptance: (1) the choice of law rules promulgated in the Restatement Second of Conflict of Laws; (2) the "governmental interest" approach developed by Professor Brainerd Currie; and (3) Professor Robert A. Leflar's theory of choice of law, in which the applicable law in multijurisdictional controversies is determined by reference to five "choice-influencing considerations." The Restatement Second approach, the product of more than a decade of research, incorporates some of the attributes of the latter two approaches, as well as others, in an attempt to "provide formulations that were true to the cases, were broad enough to permit further development in the law, and yet were able to give some guidance by pointing to what was thought would probably be the result reached in the majority of cases." * * * A majority of the courts that have abandoned lex loci have adopted the principles of the Restatement Second as representing the most comprehensive and equitably balanced approach to conflict of laws. It is therefore our conclusion that we too should incorporate the guidelines of the Restatement as the governing principles for those cases in which application of the doctrine of lex loci would produce an arbitrary, irrational result.

III

We turn now to an examination of the relevant provisions of the Restatement Second of Conflict of Laws in the context of the dispute presently before us. We note that the defendant, if he cannot persuade us to retain the doctrine of lex loci in its entirety, argues, in the alternative, that application of the principles of the Restatement would likewise require deference to the law of Quebec in the circumstances of this case. Careful analysis of the relevant Restatement provisions persuades us of the merits of the opposite conclusion.

Section 145 of the Restatement Second provides in subsection (1) that "[t]he rights and liabilities of the parties with respect to an issue are determined by the local law of the state which, with respect to that issue, has the most significant relationship to the occurrence and the parties under the principles stated in § 6." Section 6 of the Restatement, in turn, provides: "(1) A court, subject to constitutional restrictions, will follow a statutory directive of its own state on choice of law. (2) When there is no such directive, the factors relevant to the choice of the applicable rule of law include (a) the needs of the interstate and international systems, (b) the relevant policies of the forum, (c) the relevant policies of other interested states and the relative interests of those states in the determination of the particular issue, (d) the protections of justified expectations, (e) the basic policies underlying the particular field of law, (f) certainty, predictability and uniformity of result, and (g) ease in the determination and application of the law to be applied."

Applying the choice of law analysis of §§ 145 and 6 to the facts of this case involves a weighing of the relative significance of the various factors that § 6 lists. Of greatest importance for present purposes are the choices of policy emphasized in § 6(2)(b), (c) and (e). We are not today concerned with a case that offends systemic policy concerns of another state or country, nor do the facts warrant an inference of justified expectations concerning the applicability of anything other than the law of the forum. FN13 Although the principles of certainty and ease of application must be taken into account, the Restatement cautions against attaching independent weight to these auxiliary factors, noting that they are ancillary to the goal of providing rational, fair choice of law rules. As comment i to § 6 states: "In a rapidly developing area, such as choice of law, it is often more important that good rules be developed than that predictability and uniformity of result should be assured through continued adherence to existing rules." See also Restatement (Second), Conflict of Laws, § 6, comment j (policy in § 6(2)(g) should "not be overemphasized, since it is obviously of greater importance that choice-of-law rules lead to desirable results").

For assistance in our evaluation of the policy choices set out in §§ 145(1) and 6(2), we turn next to § 145(2) of the Restatement, which establishes black-letter rules of priority to facilitate the application of the principles of § 6 to tort cases. * * * Section 145(2) provides: "Contacts to be taken into account in applying the principles of § 6 to determine the law applicable to an issue include: (a) the place where the injury occurred, (b) the place where the conduct causing the injury occurred, (c) the domicile, residence, nationality, place of incorporation and place of business of the parties, and (d) the place where the relationship, if any, between the parties is centered. These contacts are to be evaluated according to their relative importance with respect to the particular issue."

In the circumstances of the present case, because the plaintiff was injured in Quebec and the tortious conduct occurred there, § 145(2)(a) and (b) weigh in favor of applying Quebec law. Because both parties are Connecticut domiciliaries and their relationship is centered here, § 145(2)(c) and (d) indicate that Connecticut law should be applied. To resolve this potential standoff, we need to recall that it is the significance, and not the number, of § 145(2) contacts that determines the outcome of the choice of law inquiry under the Restatement approach. As the concluding sentence of § 145(2) states, "[t]hese contacts are to be evaluated according to their relative importance with respect to the particular issue."

In order to apply the § 6 guidelines to the circumstances of the present case, we must, therefore, turn our attention once more to the particular issue whose disparate resolution by two relevant jurisdictions gives rise to the conflict of laws. Specifically, we must analyze the respective policies and interests of Quebec, the place of injury, and Connecticut, the forum state, with respect to the issue of whether the plaintiff should be allowed to recover damages from the defendant in a private cause of action premised on the defendant's negligent operation of an automobile. In the process of that analysis, we must evaluate the relevance of each jurisdiction's § 145(2) contacts to this particular controversy.

We first consider the policies and interests of Quebec in this regard. Quebec, as the place of injury, has an obvious interest in applying its standards of conduct to govern the liability, both civil and criminal, of persons who use its highways. * * * "This interest arises from the right and duty of the sovereign to protect those within its borders from injury to person or property...." * * * If the issue at stake in the present controversy were whether the defendant's conduct was negligent, we might well conclude that Quebec's interest in applying its law was of paramount significance. * * *

In the present case, however, the relevant Quebec law expresses no interest in regulating the conduct of the defendant, but rather limits the liability exposure to which his conduct subjects him. Quebec's Automobile Insurance Act, Quebec Revised Statutes, chapter A–25, presumably embodies policies similar to that of our own no-fault automobile insurance act: assurance to automobile accident victims of access to expeditious and adequate financial compensation, and assurance to automobile owners of access to insurance at reasonable premiums. * * * Quebec, however, has chosen to implement this policy, in title II, § 4, with a provision which, like our workers' compensation act; * * * eschews investigation into the possible negligence of the defendant's conduct and limits the amount of damages the victim of the defendant's conduct may recover. In *Reich v. Purcell,* 67 Cal.2d 551, 556, 432 P.2d 727, 63 Cal.Rptr. 31 (1967), Chief Justice Traynor, speaking with regard to statutory limitations on wrongful death damages, noted: "Limitations of damages ... have little or nothing to do with conduct. They are concerned not with how people should behave but with how survivors should be compensated. The state of the place of the wrong has little or no interest in such compensation when none of the parties reside there."

The policies behind Quebec's no-fault rule would not be substantially furthered by application of Quebec law in the circumstances of the present case. In this case, neither the victim nor the tortfeasor is a Quebec resident. There is no evidence on the record that the vehicle involved in the accident was insured or registered in Quebec. * * * Rather, the record indicates that the parties were merely "passing through" the province, and that the location of the accident was fortuitous. Clearly the goal of reducing insurance premiums in Quebec is not furthered by application of the Quebec no-fault act to an accident involving only nonresidents of Quebec, in an automobile that was not insured in the province. Quebec's interest in alleviating the administrative and judicial costs of automobile accident litigation is in no way implicated when, as in this case, a nonresident brings suit against another nonresident in a foreign jurisdiction. We note that a Quebec resident suing the defendant in Connecticut would not be subject to the Quebec act's lawsuit prohibition; under the Quebec act, such a plaintiff would be entitled to statutory compensation under Quebec law as well as any damages recoverable in a private action under Connecticut law. * * * Application of Quebec law in these circumstances would thus produce the same anomalous result that we deplored in *Simaitis v. Flood,* 182 Conn. 24, 29–30, 437 A.2d 828 (1980), since it would "bestow upon temporary visitors injured in Connecticut all the relief which [Connecticut law] affords, but deny that same relief to Connecticut residents" injured in Quebec. Id.

The foregoing analysis leads us to conclude that Quebec's status as the place of injury is not a significant contact for purposes of our choice of law inquiry in this case. Accordingly, since Quebec has no other contacts with this litigation, we hold that Quebec has no interest in applying its no-fault act to bar the plaintiff's action.

In order to justify the application of Connecticut law to the issue at stake, however, we must consider whether Connecticut's contacts with the litigation give it a legitimate interest in applying its law to the controversy. We are persuaded that Connecticut does have the requisite significant contacts.

Connecticut has a significant interest in this litigation because both the plaintiff and the defendant are, and were at the time of the accident, Connecticut domiciliaries. Consequently, to the extent that they might have anticipated being involved in an automobile accident, they could reasonably have expected to be subject to the provisions of Connecticut's no-fault act. More importantly, however, Connecticut has a strong interest in assuring that the plaintiff may avail herself of the full scope of remedies for tortious conduct that Connecticut law affords. * * * Connecticut's no-fault act serves similar purposes to Quebec's Automobile Insurance Act; * * * with one important exception: unlike the Quebec act, the Connecticut act embraces the policy of "providing the more seriously injured the opportunity to seek true redress" in a judicial forum. * * * To deny the plaintiff a cause of action in this case would frustrate this important purpose of the Connecticut no-fault statute. This is particularly true when, as in this case, the alleged consequences of the plaintiff's injury, including medical expenses and lost income, have been borne in Connecticut.

Our conclusion that we should look to the law of Connecticut rather than to the law of Quebec in this case should not be construed as a blanket endorsement of reliance on Connecticut law in all circumstances. We are persuaded that, in this case, justice and reason point to Connecticut as the jurisdiction whose laws bear the most significant relationship to the controversy at hand. We are reassured that courts in other jurisdictions, relying on the Restatement Second of Conflict of Laws, have equally concluded that they should disregard the law of a foreign jurisdiction that has at best a fortuitous and incidental relationship to the controversy to be adjudicated. * * * We can readily conceive of circumstances, however, in which the choice between the relevant jurisdictions would be much more problematic. For example, Quebec law would have been entitled to greater weight if the accident had involved a Quebec resident;* * * or a unique configuration of Quebec roads; * * * or if the defendant's negligent conduct, rather than the plaintiff's right to sue, had been at issue. The guiding principles of the Restatement command respect precisely because they encourage a searching case-by-case contextual inquiry into the significance of the interests that the law of competing jurisdictions may assert in particular controversies.

We therefore reverse the judgment of the Appellate Court upholding the trial court's granting of the motion to strike the plaintiff's complaint, and direct that this case be remanded to the trial court for further proceedings consistent with this opinion.

# CHAPTER SEVEN

# DISCOVERY

## I. INTRODUCTION

In Chapter 6, Defendant Michael Ridge hoped for a speedy resolution of the case when counsel moved to dismiss. As you saw there, the rules were designed to limit motions on the pleadings, usually, to cases where the pleader failed to state a legally recognized claim. The rules reflect a preference for allowing the parties to engage in discovery and only then to seek dismissal by way of a summary judgment. As discussed below, our system is unusual: it allows far more discovery than systems elsewhere.

For purposes of this simulation, assume that the court denied the defendant's motion to dismiss. This chapter introduces you to rules governing discovery and to exercises that allow you to engage in discovery. After a brief overview of federal discovery rules, this chapter consists of a discussion of the scope of discovery, along with some limitations on that scope, a description of the rule governing automatic disclosure of certain information and various discovery devices. It also includes several sample forms. This chapter discusses simulation exercises that your professor may assign.

## II. DISCOVERY: SOME BACKGROUND

You saw in earlier chapters the dilemma facing Ms. Nobile. She had to file her complaint without time to do a significant amount of fact-checking. But beyond that, even with resources and time to conduct an investigation, she does not have access to a great deal of information that may bear on her case. Ms. Nobile's case may be unusual because of her need for swift action. But her case is similar to many cases where the plaintiff's opponent has access to information that the plaintiff needs to prove her case. Without liberal discovery, she may not be able to prevail at trial.

Thus this case begs a question: should a litigant be able to compel her opponents or a stranger to the litigation to produce information helpful to prove *her* case? To make the point even more starkly, should a party to litigation be able to ask (and compel an answer if her opponent refuses to answer) questions that prove her opponent acted improperly or even illegally? Should she be able to ask highly personal and embarrassing questions and compel her opponent to respond?

Elsewhere, most legal systems limit discovery.[1] Most countries do not force a party to help its adversary make its case. Some countries have laws designed to frustrate American courts from forcing parties from producing documents located abroad. Even in the United States, discovery did not exist at common law. Equity allowed limited discovery. Code pleading began expanding the scope of discovery, but the drafters of the Federal Rules of Civil Procedure went further than did states adopting Code pleading.

As discussed earlier, the F.R.C.P. set the bar quite low at the pleading stage. At least prior to recent Supreme Court cases, a plaintiff could easily satisfy pleading requirements. As the rules were designed, a motion to dismiss under F.R.C.P. 12(b)(6) should be successful only upon a showing that the plaintiff's complaint does not state a legally recognized theory of recovery. The rules were designed to allow the parties to get to discovery and granted them expanded access to information.

The federal discovery rules advanced a number of important policies. Least controversial is the goal of preserving evidence, for example, where a witness may be ill or may be leaving the jurisdiction and, therefore, will be beyond the reach of the court later in the proceedings. Not especially controversial is the use of discovery to narrow issues in the case. More controversial and innovative is the decision to give litigants access to information from their opponents about their own and their opponents' cases. Although narrowed a bit in 2000, F.R.C.P. 26(b)(1), which defines the scope of discovery, provided that a party could seek discovery as long as the information was related to the subject of the dispute and reasonably calculated to lead to admissible evidence. Such liberal discovery, which takes place well before trial, eliminates the element of surprise.[2] Litigation should be about doing substantial justice and should look less like a sporting contest than it would under other systems. Liberal discovery levels the playing field for litigants unable to spend large sums on investigators. The system benefits because liberal discovery should lead to the settlement of disputes. It should also benefit the litigants, who should have an accurate assessment of the value of their respective cases.

Liberal discovery has its critics. Apart from concerns about being compelled to assist one's opponent, critics argue that discovery is subject to abuse. On occasion, when discovery makes it into media portrayals of litigation, the public is given the impression of snarky lawyers hiding documents or otherwise evading their obligation to participate in discovery. Depending on whom one is listening to, discovery abuses are common: some critics claim that plaintiffs engage in over-discovery as a way to coerce settlements while defendants engage in evasive practices to frustrate understaffed plaintiffs' lawyers.

---

1. As observed by the German Supreme Court, "... it is fundamental that no party is obligated to help its adversary to victory by furnishing him with information that he does not already have."

2. Depending on the context, surprise may be necessary. For example, when one party has a surveillance tape demonstrating that the other party has exaggerated his injuries, courts have recognized that the party attempting to compel disclosure is trying to decide whether it is safe to testify to greater injuries than she may have suffered. One solution is to time to disclosure until after the party seeking discovery has been deposed.

Empirical evidence of abuse is less condemning of the profession: discovery abuses occur in relatively few cases. But when abuse does occur, it costs litigants and the system a great deal.

The perception of abuse has driven some reform efforts. On two occasions during the 1980s and then on other occasions later, the Advisory Committee and the Court have modified the rules to address discovery abuses. Rather than wholesale reform, the drafters have increased the involvement of the judge in supervising discovery, narrowed slightly the scope of discovery, and set presumptive limits on the number of interrogatories and depositions.

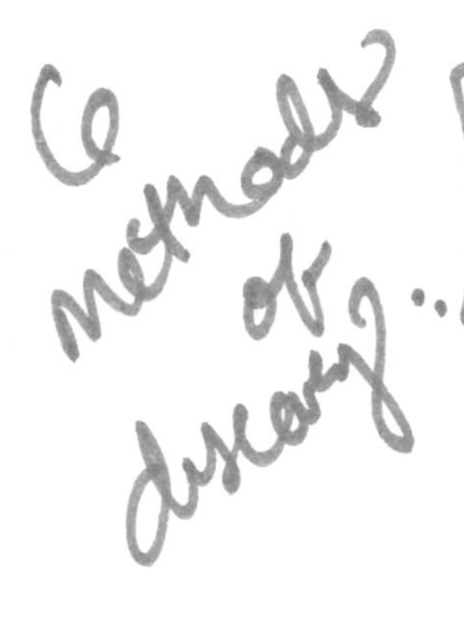

The rest of this chapter introduces you to six methods whereby parties discover information about their case: automatic disclosure, interrogatories, depositions, requests for production of documents and other tangible things, medical examinations, and requests for admissions.

## III. THE SCOPE OF DISCOVERY

F.R.C.P. 26(b)(1) provides that, "Parties may obtain discovery regarding any nonprivileged matter that is relevant to any party's claim or defense.... For good cause, the court may order discovery of any matter relevant to the subject matter involved in the action." The rule originally allowed discovery of information "relevant to the subject matter of the dispute involved in the action." Effective since December 2000, the current version is somewhat narrower. The change was motivated by the perception that plaintiffs used discovery to engage in fishing expeditions. Prior to recent Supreme Court cases that may have set a higher standard for pleading, critics of the federal rules contended that F.R.C.P. 8(a)(2) set the bar so low that a plaintiff could easily get past a motion to dismiss and then engage in extensive discovery. As you can see, the current standard narrows the scope of discovery to the claims or defenses already plead.

Especially in light of the ability of the litigants to seek a court order expanding discovery to matters relevant "to the subject matter involving in the action," one can doubt that the 2000 amendment has had much of an effect on federal practice. The decision whether to allow a broader scope of discovery is entrusted to the sound discretion of the trial court. As a result, appellate courts have not had much of a role in defining legal standards to govern such motions.

The original drafters of the rules wanted the scope of discovery to be broad for a number of reasons. Liberal discovery did more than level the playing field. Some states required litigants to show that they were requesting admissible evidence. The drafters of the rules rejected that kind of requirement, in part, to keep discovery disputes out of the courts. Although recent amendments have invited greater participation by the judge, discovery is supposed to proceed with limited judicial involvement.[3] Hence, the rules do

3. While the rules have increased the judge's role in discovery in recent years, the rules also require the parties to attempt to resolve their disputes in good faith before asking for the court's intervention in their discovery disputes. See, e.g., F.R.C.P. 26(c)(1) ("The motion must include a

not anticipate and the courts do not encourage litigants to file motions arguing whether discovery requests are for admissible evidence; litigants are supposed to await trial to make those kinds of objections.

F.R.C.P. 26(b)(1) does not allow discovery of privileged material. Parties need to object if the opposing party seeks discovery of privileged matters. Part of the point of protecting privileged communication is to avoid the embarrassment of having one's private conversations revealed. Answering discovery requests and then objecting at trial does not protect the interest served by the privilege. Answering a question concerning privileged matters may lead to the waiver of the privilege. The rules now require the party asserting the privilege to make certain representations to the court to allow an assessment whether the privilege is properly invoked. See F.R.C.P. 26(b)(5)(A).

Despite some attempts to equate privilege with admissibility, the meaning of "privilege" is well-established. The concept of "privilege" is borrowed from the law of Evidence and involves confidential communication between individuals in recognized relationships. For example, communications between attorneys and clients, between doctors and patients and between husbands and wives are recognized privileges.

"Work product" is often confused with privilege. It is a separate and more limited area where a litigant may be able to resist disclosure. Work product is broader in that it does not involve confidential communication; but it is narrower than privilege because, under some circumstances, the court may order its disclosure.

F.R.C.P. 26(b)(3) defines work product as "documents and tangible things that are prepared in anticipation of litigation or for trial." The protection applies even before an action has been filed. But even if a suit is in progress, material prepared in the ordinary course of business or pursuant to public reporting requirements are not entitled to protection under F.R.C.P. 26(b)(3). Even if a document is work product, a party seeking discovery may be able to make a sufficient showing of "substantial need" and the inability to obtain substantial equivalent of the material sought without undue hardship. Still unresolved is whether a court should ever reveal work product material that includes an attorney's mental impressions, conclusions, opinions or legal theories.

The rules also include special provisions dealing with expert witnesses. F.R.C.P. 26(a) requires parties to identify as part of automatic disclosure any expert witnesses whom the parties may use at trial. Part of that rule also requires testifying experts to prepare written reports. For reasons similar to policies supporting the work product rule, the rules also limit an opponent's ability to secure discovery concerning an expert consulted in anticipation of litigation but who will not testify.

In the 1980s, acknowledging concerns that some parties engaged in overly broad discovery in an effort to extort a settlement, the drafters of the rules modified the rules, allowing a court to consider proportionality in

certification that the movant has in good faith conferred or attempted to confer with other affected parties in an effort to resolve the dispute without court action.")

assessing a party's discovery requests. F.R.C.P. 26(b)(2)(C) requires the court to limit discovery if it finds the party's discovery request unreasonably cumulative or disproportionate. Further, the rules have created presumptive limits on the number of interrogatories and depositions that a party may take without a court order. Finally, F.R.C.P. 26(c) has always allowed a party to seek a protective order to prevent abusive discovery of various kinds.

# IV. FORMS OF DISCOVERY

## A. Automatic Disclosure

F.R.C.P. 26(a) provides that, except as exempted by the rule, without awaiting a discovery request, parties must disclose specified information to their opponents. Examine that list as part of this simulation exercise.

Automatic disclosure has a short and fascinating history. This device was added to the rules in 1993. It required the parties to hand over a great deal of information, including information harmful to their case. The supporters of the rule argued that competent lawyers would eventually succeed in discovering the information covered by the amended rule. Opponents to the rule came from a broad political spectrum including the American Civil Liberties Union and a host of business organizations. The Court divided 6–3 on whether to adopt the new device. To secure adoption, the proponents added a provision that allowed federal districts to opt out of automatic disclosure. Many districts did so.

Critics argued that the rule was contrary to our adversarial system and made a party's lawyer an instrument of that party's opponent. Further, they voiced concern about attorney-client relations: clients would not respond well to being forced to pay their lawyers for helping their opponents. They argued also that the rule would add to expense and delay.

Despite counterarguments, the rule was amended in 2000. The current rule abandons the opt-out provision. Most important, it is now limited to information that will "support [a party's] claim or defense."

For purposes of this simulation, your professor will assign you the role of representing Ms. Nobile or Mr. Ridge. S/he will give you a packet of material gathered from your client. The assignment requires you to examine Rule 26(a) and the packet of material. Figure out what information you must automatically disclose to your opponent. Also examine F.R.C.P. 26(f), which creates an obligation for the lawyers to meet and confer on various topics, including arranging for automatic disclosure and developing a discovery plan. Your professor will assign you an opponent (or opponents if your professor has students work together in groups) and will have you meet and confer and then subsequently provide your opponent with the information from your packet that is within Rule 26(a). In addition, you should work with your opponent(s) in drafting a discovery plan. Some courts have created standard forms, showing the litigants what should be included in such a discovery plan. At the end of this chapter, you will find the discovery plan form from the United States District Court for the District of New Hampshire.

You need to be familiar with the various discovery devices before you can develop your discovery plan. The following sections supplement your casebook's description of those various devices.

## B. Interrogatories

F.R.C.P 33 governs interrogatories. An interrogatory is a written question and may be directed only to another party to the litigation. Responding can be burdensome and is usually done in consultation with an attorney. As a result, litigants cannot require non-parties to respond to interrogatories. While interrogatories are useful, answers seldom produce startling revelations, largely because the answers are prepared by the party's attorney in consultation with the client. Interrogatories are helpful in garnering background and objective information. Properly used, they can shorten depositions and as a result, usually are sent in advance of taking depositions.

Interrogatories also allow a litigant to tap into the collective knowledge of her opponent. Imagine, for example, a large organization where not all employees have knowledge about the particulars of a case before the court. Deposing such individuals may not yield all the relevant information possessed by the collective entity. Interrogatories tap into the organization's collective knowledge: a party has an obligation to conduct an inquiry to respond to interrogatories.

The rule implicitly recognizes that attorneys routinely answer interrogatories. For example, since 1970, it has stated that a party may not object to an interrogatory on the ground that it calls for an opinion or application of law to fact. A lay person may not be able to specify whether she was negligent or was acting in the scope of her employment; an attorney should be able to make that determination.

In 1993, the drafters created a presumptive limit of 25 interrogatories.[4] You might wonder how parties can limit themselves to a mere 25 interrogatories. There are a few responses: the parties can agree between themselves to extend the number of interrogatories. (In fact, in a large percentage of all cases, the parties engage in informal discovery.) The rule also gives the court the authority to extend the limit. Importantly, the limitation was imposed when the drafters added the first version of automatic disclosure. As explained by proponents of automatic disclosure, parties would automatically disclose a good deal of information that might otherwise be requested through interrogatories. The 25-interrogatory limitation continues even though automatic disclosure was limited in 2000.

As discussed below, the rules also allow a party to request production of electronic recordings, documents, or other tangible things. Parties commonly include such requests as part of their interrogatories. Thus, a party may request an answer to a question and then ask the opposing party to attach any documents relevant to the answer. The practice is so common that one

---

4. As stated in the rule, each discrete subpart of an interrogatory is a separate question. On occasion, a court has had to decide the meaning of "discrete subpart."

would not likely object on the ground that the request should be made under F.R.C.P. 34.

Drafting good interrogatories is an art form. The drafter is trying to ask for as much information as possible but may not know how to describe it. Failing to describe information with sufficient detail may allow the opposing attorney to evade answering fully; describing what one seeks too specifically may allow the opposing attorney to avoid providing the information as well. Your casebook probably includes a case where the lawyers on one side of the litigation attempted to "game" the system. For a particularly egregious example, look at *Washington State Physicians Ins. Exchange & Ass'n v. Fisons Corp.*, 858 P.2d 1054 (Wash. 1993).

As with automatic disclosure, your professor will most likely have you continue representing Ms. Nobile or Mr. Ridge. S/he will have you prepare a set of interrogatories, which you will serve on your opponent. Further, s/he will have you respond to your opponent's interrogatories. In preparing your response to your opponent's interrogatories, examine not only the packet of material provided by your professor, but also consider your various options under the rules. For example, do you have adequate information to respond? Do you want to object to the whole set of interrogatories? Do the interrogatories ask for privileged material? Work product material? If so, how do you respond to avoid being in violation of F.R.C.P. 37, governing sanctions for violations of discovery rules?

## C. Production of Documents[5]

You may have seen movies like "Class Action" where one party attempts to evade discovery by hiding relevant documents in boxes filled with thousands of pages of discovery material. While a bit extreme, such portrayals capture some aspects of F.R.C.P. 34. It allows parties to request large numbers of relevant documents or other tangible things, to request entry onto land, and to have access to information electronically stored. The rule was also amended to allow similar requests to be directed to nonparties.[6]

Regulation of discovery of electronically stored information is a continuing issue for the rules' drafters. Obviously, as long as the rules allow liberal discovery, a party must have access to electronically stored data. But litigants sometimes questioned how a rule drafted long before ESI should apply to such information. The rule was amended in 2006 to make clear that ESI is within the rules. F.R.C.P. 34 has some specific provisions governing such discovery.

A party may not have documents in its possession. That is not a proper basis of objection to a request for production. The rule states that one must

**5.** Keep in mind that parties should have already either produced documents or indicated what documents the parties will rely on to prove their own claims or defenses. Thus, the focus of F.R.C.P. 34 requests is on getting documents that probably hurt one's opponent's case. That may create incentive to read the request for documents begrudgingly.

**6.** Prior to the amendment in 1991, a party seeking discovery from a nonparty had to schedule a deposition of the nonparty and direct a subpoena duces tecum to that person. The 1991 amendment now simply requires a party to direct a request to the nonparty and to comply with F.R.C.P. 45 (dealing with subpoenas).

produce documents in one's possession, control or custody. Possession and custody include constructive possession and custody. Control means that the party has a legal right to obtain the documents. For example, a corporation may have to produce documents in possession of its subsidiary.

Unless you have asked your opponents for documents as part of your interrogatories, your professor may have you send your opponents a request for documents. The rule requires the party seeking discovery to describe the thing sought "with reasonable particularity." As with interrogatories, you may have trouble describing relevant documents. That, of course, is one of the lessons that you may learn in performing this simulation exercise. Your professor may also have you respond to your opponents' request for production. Assess whether that request is sufficiently particular. In making a decision about whether a request is sufficiently particular, keep in mind that the standard is flexible, not capable of a precise definition. Also consider whether you are applying an overly technical interpretation of your opponent's request. You have also requested documents from your opponents. You create a poor impression if you have sought discovery based on a broad request for production and also resist on your narrow reading of your opponents' request. The judge has discretion in how to resolve discovery disputes and in whether to impose sanctions. Playing the rules too coyly is not a good strategy.

As with other discovery requests, you have options in how to respond. Review the rules to see your options. Consider whether you can object to the entire request for production. If you object to specific requests, consider how you make those objections. For example, how do you object that a document is protected as privileged or as work product?

## D. Depositions

F.R.C.P. 30 allows parties to take depositions of anyone with relevant information. It was amended to limit the number of depositions and the length of depositions. Those limitations are subject to a court order allowing more discovery than provided in the rule. Lawyers may differ on the ideal time to take depositions. For example, some may prefer to wait until after production of documents to make best use of the deposition. But few lawyers would dispute the reality that a deposition is the best discovery device.

Depositions have a few disadvantages. They are expensive. They may preserve evidence in a form that one's opposing party may later use at trial. Especially in light of that fact, an attorney taking a deposition may reveal a good deal about her case in her questioning of the opposing party or adverse witness.

Despite those drawbacks, depositions are extremely helpful. Unlike interrogatories, depositions allow an attorney to get spontaneous answers from the person deposed. The attorney can be flexible and pick up on information that the witness may inadvertently reveal. The deposition commits the witness to a version of the events, leaving the witness open to effective cross-examination if the witness changes her story at trial. The attorney should be able to assess the witness's credibility, a consideration relevant to the settlement value of the case.

Conducting a successful deposition is difficult. For example, the National Institute for Trial Advocacy conducts training even for experienced lawyers. This simulation can hardly make you an expert. But the simulation is designed to let you begin learning how to take an effective deposition.

Here are a few tips if your professor assigns you the role of taking or defending a deposition. Preparing for the deposition requires a careful review of all of the documents that you have gathered from your opponent and a similar review of all of the information provided by your client. By reviewing your complaint or, if you represent the defendant, by reviewing the complaint filed against your client, you should have a good idea of the relevant legal theories and facts that the plaintiff must prove to prevail at trial. Your review should give you an idea of the kinds of questions that you should prepare in advance.

If you are deposing the opposing party or hostile witness, you may make a fundamental mistake: you may treat the examination like cross-examination. Treat it like direct examination. You want to discover information. The basic rule of direct examination is to ask questions focusing on who, what, where, when and how. Asking those kinds of questions should produce relevant information. A lawyer conducting cross-examination, by comparison, asks leading questions, which assume the answer. All that you may get by asking such questions is information that you know or an answer directly opposite of the answer that you have suggested in your question.

Do not be wedded to your written questions. Instead, begin by asking the witness for some general background questions. Watch the deponent. Is he credible? Is he telling a coherent story? Let the person talk for a time and listen for any unexpected information. Some texts on how to take a winning deposition analogize the process to a funnel: start with a general discussion but then narrow the focus.

As you narrow the focus, be sure to cover the specific questions that you prepared in advance. Organize your questions in advance. You should have a reason for your sequence of questions. For example, you may want to ask a set of questions about each issue in the case. Or you may want to ask questions in chronological order. While asking specific questions, be flexible. Listen closely and follow up with additional questions that allow you to go deeper than you might otherwise go if you simply follow your script.

Almost certainly, a lawyer gets better information from a witness when she does not attack the witness. Not only is the deposition not cross-examination, but also a person who is at ease and not angry and defensive may well provide honest and helpful answers. While maintaining a professional and not hostile attitude towards the deponent, you ought to press the witness to answer questions fully. A person's initial response may be vague, but he may be willing to try to be more precise especially if you have given him an incentive to cooperate—for example, because you have been respectful. During your examination, try varying the way in which you ask questions. For example, you can leave the logical flow and go back to an earlier line of questioning to see if you can get a more spontaneous response. Try summarizing earlier testimony and see if the witness will agree with your characterization. You may want to suggest ways in which the witness was mistaken, especially if her testimony is inconsistent with other witnesses' testimony or with information you have found in documents. Finally, try to end each area of inquiry with a general question, like, "can you think of anything else about the event?"

If you are defending the deposition, you should have prepared the witness by conducting a mock deposition. The witness should be prepared and should readily admit that you and he have discussed his testimony. Not preparing your witness suggests a lack of competence on your part. During the deposition, you can make technical objections (hearsay, for example), but such questions are not objectionable during the deposition if the only basis of the objection is the form of the question. Even if you object, the attorney conducting the deposition is entitled to an answer. There are some exceptions.

During the deposition, you must object and not let your client or the witness answer if the question touches on privileged information. As discussed earlier, beginning to answer may constitute a waiver of the privilege. Beyond that, you should listen carefully to your opponent's questions. You waive an objection if you do not make it during the deposition if the basis of the objection is to the appropriateness of the question. For example, you should object to a vague or complex or misleading question. You can also object if counsel conducting the deposition becomes hostile to the witness.

The rules are designed to limit the role of the judge in the taking of a deposition. But there may come a point where counsel must object and tell her client not to answer a question. That is the case with privileged material. Where the parties cannot resolve their differences over the appropriateness of questioning, a party may seek a protective order. F.R.C.P. 30(d)(3)(A) provides that "At any time during the deposition, the deponent or a party may move to terminate or limit it on the ground that it is being conducted in bad faith or in a manner that unreasonably annoys, embarrasses, or oppresses the deponent or party."

Your professor has role summaries for some of the parties and some of the potential witnesses. That allows your professor to assign class members or research assistants those roles. As with other parts of this simulation, your professor may assign you the role of counsel for one of the parties and have you conduct part or all of a deposition.

## E. Physical or Mental Examinations

F.R.C.P. 35 allows a court to order a party to submit to various kinds of physical or mental examinations. Unlike other discovery rules, F.R.C.P. 35 anticipates involvement by the court. That is so because of privacy concerns arising from a compelled physical or psychological examination. Despite that, attorneys routinely arrange for examinations without court involvement.

Counsel for a plaintiff would be foolish to resist a request for a physical examination in a personal injury case. The plaintiff's physical condition is almost always in controversy and defense counsel does not have a hard time showing good cause for the court order. In some cases, the defendant's vision or physical abilities may be in question; there too, opposing the examination is shortsighted.

Physical and mental examinations are not appropriate in all cases. Consider the simulation. Your professor may ask you to serve as counsel for either the plaintiff or the defendant. If so, your job will be to consider whether any such examinations are appropriate and if so, to file the necessary motion to compel the examination.

## F. Admissions

F.R.C.P. 36 allows parties to seek admissions from their opponents. The rule allows a party to ask her opponent to admit or deny any relevant fact in the case or the genuineness of any document that may be used at trial. The latter part of the rule works well if the case goes to trial because it shortens the process of authenticating documents that the parties will admit into evidence.

Unlike earlier pleading systems, the federal pleading rules were not designed primarily as a way to narrow issues.[7] By the end of discovery, the parties can narrow the issues. Requests for admissions allow them to do so. They may be directed only to another party; the rules do not create a limit on the number that may be asked.

While the rule does not limit when the request may be made, such a request is best made after discovery. That should also allow parties to frame their requests more clearly. Unlike trying to ask the other party what is behind the curtain—the litigant's problem when she drafts interrogatories—she should now know what evidence is available. Well framed requests for admissions should render the next stages of the proceedings more efficient.

Your professor may have you draft a set of requests for admissions based on the information that you have discovered from your opponents during earlier parts of this chapter. Once you have received your answers, you are ready to consider whether the case is ripe for a motion for summary judgment.

7. Although some narrowing of issues occurs if a party admits allegations in the opponent's pleading, the responsive pleading comes early in the litigation before the parties have had a chance for meaningful discovery. As a practical matter, attorneys usually do not admit facts at the early stage of the litigation.

# V. FORMS

## A. Discovery Plan

Sample Discovery Plan

UNITED STATES DISTRICT COURT

DISTRICT OF NEW HAMPSHIRE

*Plaintiff(s)*

v. Civil No. Case

#/Judge Initials

*Defendant(s)*

**DISCOVERY PLAN**

**Fed. R. Civ. P. 26(f)**

**DATE/PLACE OF CONFERENCE:**

**COUNSEL PRESENT/REPRESENTING:**

**CASE SUMMARY**

**THEORY OF LIABILITY:**

**THEORY OF DEFENSE:**

**DAMAGES:**

**DEMAND:** *due date [need not be filed with the court]*

**OFFER:** *due date [need not be filed with the court]*

**JURISDICTIONAL QUESTIONS:**

**QUESTIONS OF LAW:**

**TYPE OF TRIAL: jury or bench**

**DISCOVERY**

**TRACK ASSIGNMENT:**

*EXPEDITED–6 MONTHS*

*STANDARD—12 MONTHS*

*COMPLEX—24 MONTHS*

**DISCOVERY NEEDED:**

*Give brief description of subjects on which discovery will be needed*

**MANDATORY DISCLOSURES (Fed. R. Civ. P. 26(a)(1))**

*Advise the court whether the parties have stipulated to a different method of disclosure than is required by Fed. R. Civ. P. 26(a)(1) or have agreed not to require any Rule 26(a)(1) disclosures.*

**ELECTRONIC INFORMATION DISCLOSURES (Fed. R. Civ. P. 26(f))**

*The parties should provide (a) a brief description of their proposals regarding the disclosure or discovery of electronically stored information (and/or attach a proposed order) and/or (b) identify any disputes regarding the same.*

**STIPULATION REGARDING CLAIMS OF PRIVILEGE/PROTECTION OF TRIAL PREPARATION MATERIALS (Fed. R. Civ. P. 26(f))**

*The parties should provide a brief description of the provisions of any proposed order governing claims of privilege or of protection as trial preparation material after production (and/or attach a proposed order).*

**COMPLETION OF DISCOVERY:**

*(1) Date all discovery complete [approximately 60 days prior to trial date according to Track] (2) If there are issues for early discovery, date for completion of discovery on those issues*

**INTERROGATORIES:**

A maximum of *(number)* [presumptive limit 25] interrogatories by each party to any other party. Responses due 30 days after service unless otherwise agreed to pursuant to Fed. R. Civ. P. 29.

**REQUESTS FOR ADMISSION:**

A maximum of *(number)* requests for admission by each party to any other party. Responses due 30 days after service unless otherwise agreed to pursuant to Fed. R. Civ. P. 29.

**DEPOSITIONS:**

A maximum of *(number)* [presumptive limit 10] depositions by plaintiff(s) and *(number)* [presumptive limit 10] by defendant(s).

Each deposition (other than of /name\) limited to a maximum of *(number)* [Presumptive Limit 7] hours unless extended by agreement of the parties.

**DATES OF DISCLOSURE OF EXPERTS AND EXPERTS' WRITTEN REPORTS AND SUPPLEMENTATIONS:**

**Plaintiff:** *due date* **Defendant:** *due date*

Supplementations under Rule 26(e) due *time(s) or interval(s).*

*Advise the court whether the parties have stipulated to a different form of expert report than that specified in Fed. R. Civ. P. 26(a)(2).*

**CHALLENGES TO EXPERT TESTIMONY:** *due date:* [no later than 45 days prior to trial]

**OTHER ITEMS**

**DISCLOSURE OF CLAIMS AGAINST UNNAMED PARTIES:**

*If defendant(s) claim that unnamed parties are at fault on a state law claim (see DeBenedetto v. CLD Consulting Engineers, Inc., 153 N.H. 793 (2006)), defendant(s) shall disclose the identity of every such party and the basis of the allegation of fault no later than [no later than 30 days before the Joinder of Additional Parties deadline and 45 days before the Plaintiff's Expert Disclosure deadline]. Plaintiff shall then have 30 days from the date of disclosure to amend the complaint.*

**JOINDER OF ADDITIONAL PARTIES:**

**Plaintiff:** *due date* **Defendant:** *due date*

**THIRD-PARTY ACTIONS:** *due date*

**AMENDMENT OF PLEADINGS:**

**Plaintiff:** *due date* **Defendant:** *due date*

**DISPOSITIVE MOTIONS:**

**To Dismiss:** *due date [no later than 90 days after preliminary pretrial]*

**For Summary Judgment:** *due date [no later than 120 days prior to trial date according to track. The fact that the discovery deadline may post-date the summary judgment deadline is not a sufficient basis to request a continuance of the summary judgment deadline.]*

**SETTLEMENT POSSIBILITIES:**

1. is likely
2. is unlikely
3. cannot be evaluated prior to (date)
4. may be enhanced by ADR:
    a. Request to the court
    b. Outside source

**JOINT STATEMENT RE MEDIATION:**

*The parties shall indicate a date by which mediation, if any, will occur.*

**WITNESSES AND EXHIBITS:** [No dates necessary; due dates–10 days before final pretrial conference but not less than 30 days before trial for lists (included in final pretrial statements) and 14 days after service of final pretrial statement for objections—set by clerk's notice of trial assignment.]

**TRIAL ESTIMATE:** *number of days*

**TRIAL DATE:**

*The parties shall set out an agreed trial date-adhering to time periods as mandated by the chosen track assignment—using a preset jury selection day as provided on the court's web site*

*(www.nhd.uscourts.gov). If the parties cannot agree on a date, they shall set out their respective proposed dates,*

**PRELIMINARY PRETRIAL CONFERENCE:**

The parties [request] [do not request] a preliminary pretrial conference with the court before entry of the scheduling order. [NOTE: The parties should plan to attend the preliminary pretrial conference as scheduled unless otherwise notified by the court.]

**OTHER MATTERS:**

*The parties should list here their positions on any other matters which should be brought to the court's attention including other orders that should be entered under Fed. R. Civ. P. 26(c) or 16(b) and (c).*

## B. Sample Interrogatories[8]

In a typical set of interrogatories, counsel includes a set of instructions. For example, under the caption Instructions, a party may direct the responding party that "Each Interrogatory is to be answered fully on the basis of information that is in your possession." Or the instructions may include a reminder that the responding party has an obligation to conduct a reasonable investigation, including, seeking information within that party's possession, custody or control. A set of interrogatories may do so by instructing the responding party to furnish information available to the responding party, and "also such information as is known to any of the agency's agents, representatives, employees, servants, consultants, contractors, subcontractors, investigators, attorneys, and any other person or entity acting or purporting to act on behalf of the agency."

Another sample instruction might remind the responding party of its obligation to file supplementary answers if that party obtains further or different information before trial. Instructions may also include a reminder of the responding party's obligation to state that party's reasons for declining to respond to a particular interrogatory.

Thereafter, counsel should provide definitions of any terms likely to cause uncertainty. Thus, in sending a set of interrogatories to a department of the government, counsel might define "person, persons, people, or individual" as "any natural person, together with all federal, state, county, municipal and other governmental units, agencies, public bodies, as well as firms, companies, corporations, partnerships, proprietorships, joint ventures, organizations, groups of natural persons or other associations or entities separately identifiable whether or not such associations or entities have a separate legal existence of their own." Commonly, counsel propounding interrogatories

---

8. You can find many more sample interrogatories on-line. A Google search for "sample interrogatories" will provide numerous sites.

defines the term "document" broadly. For example, a set of interrogatories may include a definition as follows: " 'document' or 'documents' are used herein in their broadest sense and includes any original, reproduction or copy of any kind, typed, recorded, graphic, printed, written or documentary matter, including without limitation correspondence, memoranda, interoffice communications, notes, diaries, contracts, drawings, plans, specifications, estimates, vouchers, permits, written ordinances, minutes of meetings, invoices, billings, checks, notes pertaining to any tangible thing, and any form of communication or representation, including letters, words, pictures, sounds or symbols or combinations thereof."

Definitions like these demonstrate the drafter's intent to prevent the opponent from trying to play games in responding by quibbling with whether, in the previous example, something is a "document." These and other similar definitions suggest that, over time, attorneys expand definitions in light of problems encountered in litigation. Finally, when you begin practice, you ought to look for standard definitions and interrogatories. As with many areas of the law, you do not have to invent, here, definitions without any guidance.

As discussed above, attorneys use interrogatories to collect objective data. Hence, in a negligence action, a defendant might ask (if the plaintiff has not provided the information as part of automatic disclosure), "identify by full name, address, and telephone number all witnesses who may have information about the cause of the accident involved in this action. State the nature of the facts known by each such person." A defendant may want to learn if the plaintiff has received compensation for some or all of her damages. In such a case, a standard form interrogatory might ask the plaintiff: "List the style and civil action number of any pending or previously adjudicated related cases." If the defendant wants to assess the economic value of a case, counsel may send an interrogatory pinning down the extent of the plaintiff's injuries. For example, it might state, "if you contend you have been injured or damaged, provide a separate statement for each item of damage, the dollar amount claimed, and citation to the statute, rule, regulation or case law authorizing a recovery for that particular item of damage." To be sure that the plaintiff has named the right party, she might ask, "if you contend that some other person or legal entity is, in whole or in part, liable for the plaintiff's injuries, state the full name, address, and telephone number of such person or entity and describe in detail why that other person or entity may be liable to the plaintiff." Or similarly, an interrogatory might ask, "if you contend that the personal injuries of Plaintiff was not caused by the collision with your vehicle, state with particularity the facts upon which you base your conclusion."

Despite the limitations of interrogatories, counsel can try to get her opponent to commit to a particular account of critical events. Thus, in an action for negligence, to comply with the forms, a plaintiff needs to allege only that the defendant acted negligently (in a particular place and at a particular time). But the defendant may try to discover how the plaintiff contends the defendant was negligent. Thus, defense counsel may ask, "Please give a concise statement of facts as to how you contend the car accident took place." In trying to determine whether the defendant has a defense of contributory negligence, counsel may ask questions like these: "Please state whether you consumed any drugs, medicines, or alcoholic beverages within 24 hours prior to the occurrence that gave rise to your complaint," "Please list all prior motor vehicle accidents in which you have been involved, either with others persons or property. Please include the name of any other driver or property owner involved, the location of the collision, the date and time of the collision, and disposition of the matter," or "Please state whether the vehicle of the Plaintiff was moving at the time of the accident, and if so, state the direction and speed of said vehicle."

An attorney may track the complaint or answer in asking interrogatories. Thus, a defendant may ask the plaintiff to "state all facts on which you base the allegations in paragraph X of your complaint." Or a plaintiff may ask similar interrogatories with regard to an affirmative defense in the answer. The plaintiff may ask the defendant to explain the facts upon which he bases his claim that the plaintiff assumed the risk.

Finally, as mentioned above, lawyers commonly include a request for documents as part of the interrogatories, instead of adding a separate request under F.R.C.P. 34. Hence, an interrogatory may state, "Identify and attach any and all documents that relate to your hiring and retention policies."

## C. Requests for Documents

As with interrogatories, attorneys include instructions and definitions in their requests for production of documents. Thus, a request for production may include language like the following: "The documents shall be produced as they are covered in the usual course of business or you shall organize and label them to correspond with the categories in the request," "These requests shall encompass all items within your possession, custody or control," and "These requests are continuing in character so as to require you to promptly amend or supplement your response if you obtain further material information." Some attorneys use an instruction intended to prevent their opponents from hiding behind ambiguity in the request for documents. Thus, counsel may state the following: "If in responding to these requests you encounter any ambiguity in construing any request, set for the matter deemed ambiguous in the construction used, in responding."

A party may make requests like the following: "Please produce all documents referred to and relied upon by you in answering your interrogatories." One may ask for "any and all photographs taken by you or any person on your behalf of the scene of the occurrence alleged in the Complaint," or "copies of all reports and written data/information taken from all persons who have any knowledge of the occurrence alleged in the Complaint."

Unlike interrogatories, requests for production of documents can be directed to a non-party. If so, the party seeking discovery serves the request for documents with a subpoena *duces tecum*. Courts may make available standard forms. Here is a sample:

AO 88A (Rev. 06/09) Subpoena to Testify at a Deposition in a Civil Action (Page 2)

Civil Action No.

PROOF OF SERVICE

***(This section should not be filed with the court unless required by Fed. R. Civ. P. 45.)***

This subpoena for *(name of individual and title, if any)*

was received by me on *(date)* ______________ .

❐ I served the subpoena by delivering a copy to the named individual as follows: ____________________

______________________________________________________________________

__________________________________________ on *(date)* __________ ; or

❐ I returned the subpoena unexecuted because: ____________________________

______________________________________________________________________ .

Unless the subpoena was issued on behalf of the United States, or one of its officers or agents, I have also tendered to the witness fees for one day's attendance, and the mileage allowed by law, in the amount of

$ ____________________ .

My fees are $ ______________ for travel and $ ____________ for services, for a total of $ 0.00 .

I declare under penalty of perjury that this information is true.

Date: ______________ ______________________________________________

*Server's signature*

______________________________________________

*Printed name and title*

______________________________________________

*Server's address*

Additional information regarding attempted service, etc:

AO 88A (Rev. 06/09) Subpoena to Testify at a Deposition in a Civil Action (Page 3)

## Federal Rule of Civil Procedure 45 (c), (d), and (e) (Effective 12/1/07)

**(c) Protecting a Person Subject to a Subpoena.**

**(1)** ***Avoiding Undue Burden or Expense; Sanctions.*** A party or attorney responsible for issuing and serving a subpoena must take reasonable steps to avoid imposing undue burden or expense on a person subject to the subpoena. The issuing court must enforce this duty and impose an appropriate sanction — which may include lost earnings and reasonable attorney's fees — on a party or attorney who fails to comply.

**(2)** ***Command to Produce Materials or Permit Inspection.***

**(A)** *Appearance Not Required.* A person commanded to produce documents, electronically stored information, or tangible things, or to permit the inspection of premises, need not appear in person at the place of production or inspection unless also commanded to appear for a deposition, hearing, or trial.

**(B)** *Objections.* A person commanded to produce documents or tangible things or to permit inspection may serve on the party or attorney designated in the subpoena a written objection to inspecting, copying, testing or sampling any or all of the materials or to inspecting the premises or to producing electronically stored information in the form or forms requested. The objection must be served before the earlier of the time specified for compliance or 14 days after the subpoena is served. If an objection is made, the following rules apply:

**(i)** At any time, on notice to the commanded person, the serving party may move the issuing court for an order compelling production or inspection.

**(ii)** These acts may be required only as directed in the order, and the order must protect a person who is neither a party nor a party's officer from significant expense resulting from compliance.

**(3)** ***Quashing or Modifying a Subpoena.***

**(A)** *When Required.* On timely motion, the issuing court must quash or modify a subpoena that:

**(i)** fails to allow a reasonable time to comply;

**(ii)** requires a person who is neither a party nor a party's officer to travel more than 100 miles from where that person resides, is employed, or regularly transacts business in person — except that, subject to Rule 45(c)(3)(B)(iii), the person may be commanded to attend a trial by traveling from any such place within the state where the trial is held;

**(iii)** requires disclosure of privileged or other protected matter, if no exception or waiver applies; or

**(iv)** subjects a person to undue burden.

**(B)** *When Permitted.* To protect a person subject to or affected by a subpoena, the issuing court may, on motion, quash or modify the subpoena if it requires:

**(i)** disclosing a trade secret or other confidential research, development, or commercial information;

**(ii)** disclosing an unretained expert's opinion or information that does not describe specific occurrences in dispute and results from the expert's study that was not requested by a party; or

**(iii)** a person who is neither a party nor a party's officer to incur substantial expense to travel more than 100 miles to attend trial.

**(C)** *Specifying Conditions as an Alternative.* In the circumstances described in Rule 45(c)(3)(B), the court may, instead of quashing or modifying a subpoena, order appearance or production under specified conditions if the serving party:

**(i)** shows a substantial need for the testimony or material that cannot be otherwise met without undue hardship; and

**(ii)** ensures that the subpoenaed person will be reasonably compensated.

**(d) Duties in Responding to a Subpoena.**

**(1)** ***Producing Documents or Electronically Stored Information.*** These procedures apply to producing documents or electronically stored information:

**(A)** *Documents.* A person responding to a subpoena to produce documents must produce them as they are kept in the ordinary course of business or must organize and label them to correspond to the categories in the demand.

**(B)** *Form for Producing Electronically Stored Information Not Specified.* If a subpoena does not specify a form for producing electronically stored information, the person responding must produce it in a form or forms in which it is ordinarily maintained or in a reasonably usable form or forms.

**(C)** *Electronically Stored Information Produced in Only One Form.* The person responding need not produce the same electronically stored information in more than one form.

**(D)** *Inaccessible Electronically Stored Information.* The person responding need not provide discovery of electronically stored information from sources that the person identifies as not reasonably accessible because of undue burden or cost. On motion to compel discovery or for a protective order, the person responding must show that the information is not reasonably accessible because of undue burden or cost. If that showing is made, the court may nonetheless order discovery from such sources if the requesting party shows good cause, considering the limitations of Rule 26(b)(2)(C). The court may specify conditions for the discovery.

**(2)** ***Claiming Privilege or Protection.***

**(A)** *Information Withheld.* A person withholding subpoenaed information under a claim that it is privileged or subject to protection as trial-preparation material must:

**(i)** expressly make the claim; and

**(ii)** describe the nature of the withheld documents, communications, or tangible things in a manner that, without revealing information itself privileged or protected, will enable the parties to assess the claim.

**(B)** *Information Produced.* If information produced in response to a subpoena is subject to a claim of privilege or of protection as trial-preparation material, the person making the claim may notify any party that received the information of the claim and the basis for it. After being notified, a party must promptly return, sequester, or destroy the specified information and any copies it has; must not use or disclose the information until the claim is resolved; must take reasonable steps to retrieve the information if the party disclosed it before being notified; and may promptly present the information to the court under seal for a determination of the claim. The person who produced the information must preserve the information until the claim is resolved.

**(e) Contempt.** The issuing court may hold in contempt a person who, having been served, fails without adequate excuse to obey the subpoena. A nonparty's failure to obey must be excused if the subpoena purports to require the nonparty to attend or produce at a place outside the limits of Rule 45(c)(3)(A)(ii).

AO 88A (Rev. 06/09) Subpoena to Testify at a Deposition in a Civil Action

# UNITED STATES DISTRICT COURT

for the

______________________________
*Plaintiff*
v.
______________________________
*Defendant*

Civil Action No.

(If the action is pending in another district, state where: )

## SUBPOENA TO TESTIFY AT A DEPOSITION IN A CIVIL ACTION

To:

❒ *Testimony:* **YOU ARE COMMANDED** to appear at the time, date, and place set forth below to testify at a deposition to be taken in this civil action. If you are an organization that is *not* a party in this case, you must designate one or more officers, directors, or managing agents, or designate other persons who consent to testify on your behalf about the following matters, or those set forth in an attachment:

| Place: | Date and Time: |
|---|---|

The deposition will be recorded by this method: ______________________________

❒ *Production:* You, or your representatives, must also bring with you to the deposition the following documents, electronically stored information, or objects, and permit their inspection, copying, testing, or sampling of the material:

The provisions of Fed. R. Civ. P. 45(c), relating to your protection as a person subject to a subpoena, and Rule 45 (d) and (e), relating to your duty to respond to this subpoena and the potential consequences of not doing so, are attached.

Date: ____________

*CLERK OF COURT*

OR

*Signature of Clerk or Deputy Clerk* *Attorney's signature*

The name, address, e-mail, and telephone number of the attorney representing *(name of party)* ______________ ______________________________, who issues or requests this subpoena, are:

## D. Requests for Admissions

Technically, requests for admissions are not a form of discovery. Although the rule does not require any particular timing for when parties make such requests, the drafters of the rules envisioned the use of requests for admissions as a post-discovery device. Having completed discovery, the parties should be in a position to narrow issues for trial. F.R.C.P. 36 facilitates that process. Again, because the parties should have a good idea of the evidence that will be available at trial, they can draft quite specific requests for admissions. I have included a few examples below.

Assume that in a torts case, the plaintiff has sued a corporate defendant for negligent acts of Driver, its employee. During discovery, the plaintiff may have learned various facts about events that occurred before the accident. Requesting the defendant to admit those facts may facilitate trial. So she may ask, "Admit that Driver drank two beers with his lunch on the day of the accident," or "Admit that Driver failed to negotiate a turn on Main Street immediately before the accident," or "Admit that Driver was driving at 35 MPH in a 25 MPH zone," or "Admit that the roadway was wet from a rain storm that occurred within one hour before the accident."

One can ask her opponent to admit that the opponent lacks evidence as well. Thus, one might ask, "Admit that the Plaintiff has no evidence that Defendant's Driver was inattentive at the moment of impact," or "Admit that the Plaintiff has no evidence that Driver drove through a red light before the collision that gave rise to this litigation."

The previous examples all involve straightforward requests dealing with facts. But as with interrogatories, parties may not object on the basis that a request for an admission calls for opinions or conclusions of law. Thus, the defendant may claim that Driver was not acting within the course and scope of his employment and/or may claim that Driver was not negligent. If during the course of discovery, the plaintiff has been able to discover evidence supporting a claim that the employee was acting within the course and scope of employment, she may direct a request for admission on that point. That request may state: "Admit that Driver was acting with the course and scope of his employment on November 1, YR-02, when he was involved in the incident giving rise to this litigation." In addition, although the defendant may deny the request for the admission, the plaintiff may also ask for an admission of liability: "Admit that Driver was negligently operating Defendant's truck when it collided with Plaintiff's vehicle on November 1, YR-02." Similar requests may seek an admission that Driver's conduct was the proximate cause of the accident or that the plaintiff did not contribute to her injuries.

# CHAPTER EIGHT

# AMENDING THE COMPLAINT

## I. INTRODUCTION

Earlier, you saw a problem that Ms. Nobile faced in filing her action. Without an opportunity for discovery and with little time for investigation, she had no idea who in the Doddville Police Department may have been responsible for leaking information about the search of Judge Elliot's office. As a result, her complaint named "unnamed officers" of the Doddville Police Department as defendants.

This chapter introduces you to F.R.C.P. 15, dealing with amendments to pleadings. It focuses on what happens when a litigant learns the identity of a previously unknown party. Further, it explores whether, in this case, Ms. Nobile can amend her complaint to name previously unknown individuals. That leads to a difficult legal question: what happens if the statute of limitations has run before a litigant moves to amend the complaint? In answering that, you will discover interplay of federal and state law. This chapter consists of material that Ms. Nobile learned during discovery, a description of the simulation exercise, and cases relevant to the legal issues presented in the simulation.

## II. LEARNING THE IDENTITIES OF UNKNOWN PARTIES

In Chapter 6, Ms. Nobile filed her complaint in the United States District Court for the District of Connecticut. For purposes of this chapter, assume that Ms. Nobile filed the complaint found in Chapter Six in the United States District Court for the District of Connecticut. In addition, assume that she added to the list of defendants named in her complaint "John Does 1–100."

In her complaint, Ms. Nobile claimed violations of federal and state law. Prior to filing her complaint, she did not know who leaked information concerning the search of Judge Elliot's chambers. Some states allow "John/Jane Doe" pleading, whereby a litigant may toll the statute of limitations by filing a claim against John or Jane Doe. The federal rules include a provision that allows "relation back" under limited circumstances. You will need to review F.R.C.P. 15(c) for purposes of this simulation.

Concerned about naming as of yet unknown defendants, Ms. Nobile's attorney attempted to discover that information through interrogatories and depositions. For purposes of this chapter, over three and a half years have passed since the filing of the complaint. Armed with information learned during discovery, the Plaintiffs attorney hopes to amend her complaint to name the previously unknown defendants and to serve them with process. Here is the relevant information learned in discovery.

## A. Relevant Interrogatories

**Plaintiffs Interrogatory #14:** How many officers are employed by the Doddville Police Department?

**Defendant's Answer to Plaintiff's Interrogatory #14: 116**

**Plaintiff's Interrogatory #15:** After receiving the complaint in this action, what actions did the Doddville Police Department take to learn which officers may have been involved in revealing contents of the sealed search warrant for Judge John Elliot's chambers?

**Defendant's Answer to Plaintiff's Interrogatory #15:** Upon receipt of the complaint, the matter was referred to the Doddville City Attorney's Office, which defends this department in civil rights litigation. Because the complaint also alleged a violation of internal policies, the matter was referred to Internal Affairs.

**Plaintiff's Interrogatory #16:** Has this matter has been investigated by the Doddville Police Department's Internal Affairs Division? If so, please attach any reports or other documents indicating the results of that investigation.

**Defendant's Answer to Plaintiff's Interrogatory #16:** The matter is under investigation and no report or other documents have resulted from that investigation.

## B. The First Deposition

After receiving answers to interrogatories, counsel for the Plaintiff arranged to take the deposition of a number of members of the police department. The first was the deposition of Norman Caplan, Chief of the Doddville Police Department. The following colloquy took place during that deposition, taken YR-03:

* * * BY MS. CONNELL: Chief Caplan, what did you do when you received the complaint in this case; specifically, did you take any steps to identify who may have leaked information about the search of Judge Elliot's chambers?

A. Of course. We have standard procedures in place in such cases.

Q. Specifically?

A. Initially, we gave the City Attorney's Office the complaint.

Q. Because?

A. Attorneys in that office represent the department in civil rights cases.

Q. Did you do anything else to learn who leaked information?

A. We did.

Q. What did you do, specifically?

A. The conduct alleged—if true—would be a violation of our internal regulations. So, after discussing the matter with the City Attorney's Office,

BY COUNSEL FOR THE DODDVILLE POLICE DEPARTMENT: May I interrupt for a moment?

BY MS. CONNELL: Of course.

BY COUNSEL FOR THE DPD: We are getting into conversations with your attorney, Chief. Let's be clear that this is not a waiver of privileged communications.

BY MS. CONNELL: For the record, I don't think that was the case—at least not at this point. May we continue, Chief?

A. Sure. The question was?

Q. After the discussion with the City Attorney's Office, did you make inquiry into whether someone in the department violated your internal regulations?

A. Well, we referred the matter to Internal Affairs.

Q. What did Internal Affairs do, what kind of investigation did it do and what did it learn?

BY COUNSEL FOR THE DPD: Objection. This is not information within the Chief's personal knowledge.

BY MS. CONNELL: That is a trial objection—not for the deposition.

BY COUNSEL FOR THE DPD: My objection is on the record.

BY MS. CONNELL: Duly noted. And Chief Caplan, do you have personal knowledge of what the Internal Affairs division did?

A. Well, yes and no.

Q. By that you mean, what?

A. The head of IA reports back to me, of course.

Q. So you have kept track what IA has learned?

A. Yes.

Q. So what did Internal Affairs do?

A. Internal Affairs called in officers who they thought might have been involved.

Q. By the way, when did they do this?

A. Within a month or six weeks after we got word that the department had been sued.

Q. Has Internal Affairs learned who might be involved?

A. Well, no but proceedings are ongoing.

Q. Has IA been able to identify anyone?

A. Not at this point, but it is interviewing everyone who had access to the search warrant.

Q. Well, I am going to finish up on this topic for now. I want to remind you of your obligation to update your responses when you have further information on this matter.

A. As you wish, counselor. * * *

## C. Ongoing Discovery

As you can see, the Plaintiff's counsel took this deposition in YR-03, about six months after suit was filed. A month ago, concerned that she had yet to receive any additional information about the identity of the officers who leaked information, Ms. Connell sent counsel for the Doddville Police Department a letter reminding him of his obligation to supplement answers to earlier discovery requests. A few days ago, counsel sent Ms. Connell a set of supplemental answers to the Plaintiff's Interrogatories. That set of supplemental answers included the following updates:

**Defendant's Supplemental Response to Plaintiffs Interrogatory #16:** The Internal Affairs division is involved in an ongoing investigation of the suspected leak involved in this lawsuit. It has yet to conclude that investigation. Find a copy of its interim report attached hereto.

Here is the relevant excerpt from that report:[0088]

Interim findings: * * *

18. Eight officers were involved in swearing out and/or executing the search warrant involved in this litigation.

19. Interviews with those officers failed to result in the identification of who may have leaked information to the Defendant Michael Ridge.

20. Telephone records reveal that three officers have had telephone contact with Ridge. Those officers are Patrolman Jeremy Coleman; Sergeant Terrance Miranda; and Detective Ernest Mapp. * * *

# III. THE SIMULATION: AMENDING THE COMPLAINT

At this point, the Plaintiffs attorney is eager to amend the complaint to add as defendants the three named officers. Examine F.R.C.P. 15. There, you will see that, because of the timing of the attempted amendment, the Plaintiff must file a motion to amend the complaint. See F.R.C.P. 15(a)(2) (requiring leave of court). Because so much of her complaint relies on her claim under § 1983, that should be the focus of this simulation. Your professor has a number of options in how to handle this simulation. For example, s/he may have you write a memorandum explaining whether the Plaintiff can successfully amend her complaint to add the three officers as named defendants. Alternatively, s/he may assign you the role of counsel for one of the parties and have you argue the issue to the judge. Or s/he may have you serve as the law clerk to the judge before whom the matter is pending and have you explain how the judge should rule on the Plaintiff's motion to amend the complaint.

Apart from the way in which your professor makes this assignment, the simulation requires you to sort through a number of problems: you must determine whether the statute of limitations has run; if so, you must determine whether the Plaintiff can invoke the benefit of the relation back provisions found within F.R.C.P. 15(c). The next section consists of cases that you should rely on in sorting out the legal questions posed by this simulation.

# IV. THE CRAZY QUILT OR THE RELEVANT CASE LAW

## A. Relying on F.R.C.P. 15(c)(1)(A)

In sorting out the questions posed in this simulation, you should consider whether the following three cases provide any help for the Plaintiff. Specifically, do they bring the facts within F.R.C.P. 15(c)(1)(A)?

### TARNOWSKY v. SOCCI

856 A.2d 408 (Conn. 2004)

SULLIVAN, C.J.

The defendant, Peter Socci, appeals from the judgment of the Appellate Court reversing the judgment of the trial court that the negligence action brought by the plaintiff, Joseph Tarnowsky, was barred by General Statutes § 52–584.[1] The Appellate Court held that the two year statute of limitations for bringing a negligence action does not begin to run until a plaintiff knows, or reasonably should have known, the tortfeasor's identity. We affirm the judgment of the Appellate Court.

The record reveals the following undisputed facts and procedural history. On March 14, 1997, the plaintiff sustained injuries when he slipped and fell on an icy sidewalk on property in Darien. In December, 1998, the plaintiff timely commenced separate negligence actions against People's Bank (bank),

1. General Statutes § 52–584 provides: "No action to recover damages for injury to the person, or to real or personal property, caused by negligence, or by reckless or wanton misconduct, or by malpractice of a physician, surgeon, dentist, podiatrist, chiropractor, hospital or sanatorium, shall be brought but within two years from the date when the injury is first sustained or discovered or in the exercise of reasonable care should have been discovered, and except that no such action may be brought more than three years from the date of the act or omission complained of, except that a counterclaim may be interposed in any such action any time before the pleadings in such action are finally closed."

the owner of the property, and Jana, LLC (Jana), the tenant of the property. Thereafter, the plaintiff learned through the formal discovery process that the defendant had been responsible for removing ice and snow from the bank's property and, on March 10, 2000, commenced this negligence action against him. On August 9, 2000, the defendant filed an apportionment complaint against the bank, Jana and Leggat McCall Properties Management of Connecticut, Inc. (Leggat). The plaintiff late amended his complaint, pursuant to General Statutes § 52–102b, to assert a direct claim against Leggat. The defendant and Leggat then filed separate motions for summary judgment, claiming that the plaintiffs claim was barred by § 52–584. The trial court … granted the defendant's motion for summary judgment … The plaintiff appealed … and the Appellate Court reversed the judgment of the trial court, holding that "actual or constructive knowledge of the identity of a tortfeasor is an essential element of a claimant's action for damages for negligently inflicted injuries" This court granted certification, limited to the following issue: "Did the Appellate Court properly conclude that the plaintiffs action against the named defendant was not barred by General Statutes § 52–584?" … * * * *

The defendant argues that knowledge of the identity of the tortfeasor is not an essential element of a cause of action and, therefore, under *Catz,* such knowledge is not required in order for the plaintiff to have suffered actionable harm. We disagree.

Whether a plaintiff has suffered actionable harm before discovering the tortfeasor's identity is an issue of first impression for this court. In *Catz,* we concluded that the discovery of the causal connection between the breach of duty and the injury was an essential element of a cause of action, but had no occasion to address the specific question before us here….

The decisions of our sibling states on the question before us are divided. The majority of those jurisdictions have held, however, that a cause of action does not accrue until the plaintiff has discovered or should have discovered the identity of the tortfeasor. See, e.g., *Siragusa v. Brown,* 114 Nev. 1384, 1393–94, 971 P.2d 801 (1998) ("trier of fact must determine whether [plaintiffs] discovery of [defendant's] involvement was delayed due to her alleged attempts to conceal her role and whether [plaintiff] could have, nonetheless, discovered her identity earlier through diligent inquiry"); *Adams v. Oregon State Police,* 289 Or. 233, 239, 611 P.2d 1153 (1980) (statute of limitations "does not commence to run until plaintiff has a reasonable opportunity to discover his injury and *the identity of the party responsible for that injury"* [emphasis added]); *Wyatt v. A—Best, Co.,* 910 S.W.2d 851, 855 (Tenn.1995) ("breach of a legally cognizable duty occurs when plaintiff discovers or 'reasonably should have discovered, (1) the occasion, the manner and means by which a breach of duty occurred that produced … injury; and (2) *the identity of the defendant who breached the duty'* " [emphasis added]); *Spitler v. Dean,* 148 Wis.2d 630, 636, 436 N.W.2d 308 (1989) (plaintiffs "cause of action did not accrue *until [he] knew the identity of the defendant,* or in the exercise of reasonable diligence, should have discovered the identity of the defendant" [emphasis added]).

We agree with the Appellate Court and the majority of our sibling jurisdictions that there is no principled reason to distinguish between, on the one hand, the discovery of a breach of duty or the discovery of a causal connection between the breach of duty and the injury and, on the other hand, the discovery of the identity of the tortfeasor, for purposes of the actionable harm doctrine...

We note that General Statutes § 52–45a provides that "[c]ivil actions shall be commenced by legal process consisting of a writ of summons or attachment, *describing the parties....*" (Emphasis added.) Unlike some jurisdictions, Connecticut has no statutory provision for suing an unidentified "John Doe" defendant.[2] In any event, a plaintiff who has incurred an actionable injury and knows the identity of one or more of the tortfeasors, but has no reason to suspect the existence of additional responsible parties, clearly cannot bring an action against the unknown parties until he discovers their existence. In such cases, the blameless failure to discover the existence of the unknown tortfeasors is tantamount to a blameless failure to discover a causal connection between the tortfeasor's breach of duty and the injury, a failure that clearly tolls the statute of limitations.... * * * *

The defendant also argues that our interpretation "turns [§ 52–584] on its head" by making the three year repose period the rule rather than the exception. We disagree. Just as the rule that we adopted in *Catz* applies only when the plaintiff did not know and reasonably could not have known of the causal connection between the breach of duty and the injury, the rule that we adopt in this case applies only when the plaintiff did not know, and reasonably could not have known, the identity of the tortfeasor. We trust that such cases are the exception, not the general rule. For the same reason, we are not persuaded by the defendant's argument that our interpretation will inject "an additional issue of fact ... into *every* negligence case that involves a statute of limitations defense." (Emphasis added.)

We also are not persuaded by the defendant's argument that our interpretation undermines the objectives of statutes of limitations and repose. We fully recognize that "[a] statute of limitation or of repose is designed to (1) prevent the unexpected enforcement of stale and fraudulent claims by allowing persons after the lapse of a reasonable time, to plan their affairs with a reasonable degree of certainty, free from the disruptive burden of protracted and unknown potential liability, and (2) to aid in the search for truth that may be impaired by the loss of evidence, whether by death or disappearance of witnesses, fading memories, disappearance of documents or otherwise." (Internal quotation marks omitted.) *DeLeo v. Nusbaum,* 263 Conn. 588,596,821 A.2d 744 (2003). As in *Catz,* our decision in this case merely recognizes that in cases in which a plaintiff, through no fault of his own and despite the exercise of reasonable care, is ignorant of an essential jurisdictional fact, the three year repose period represents a legislative compromise between the public policy of protecting individuals from the uncertainty that

2. For example, California law provides that "[w]hen the plaintiff is ignorant of the name of a defendant, he must state that fact in the complaint ... and such defendant may be designated ... by any name...." Cal.Civ.Proc.Code § 474 (Deering Sup.2004).

could result from unduly protracted time limits for filing legal claims and the public policy favoring the vindication of meritorious claims in the courts....

We conclude that the two year statute of limitations set forth in § 52–584 does not begin to run until a plaintiff knows, or reasonably should have known, the identity of the tortfeasor. We emphasize that a plaintiffs ignorance of the identity of a tortfeasor will not excuse the plaintiffs failure to bring a negligence action within three years of the date of the act or omission complained of. When the plaintiff in the present case knew or should have known the defendant's identity is a question to be determined by the fact finder on remand.

The judgment of the Appellate Court is affirmed.

## LOUNSBURY v. JEFFRIES

25 F.3d 131 (2nd Cir. 1994)

KEARSE, CIRCUIT JUDGE:

Plaintiffs Linda Lounsbury and William R. Donaldson, Jr., appeal from a judgment entered in the United States District Court for the District of Connecticut, Peter C. Dorsey, *Judge,* summarily dismissing their consolidated action, brought under 42 U.S.C. § 1983 (1988) for false arrest, on the ground that their complaints were barred by Connecticut's two-year statute of limitations. On appeal, plaintiffs contend that the state's three-year statute should have been applied, and that, under the proper statute, their suits were timely filed. We agree, and we therefore reverse and remand for further proceedings.

### I. BACKGROUND

The facts, taken in the light most favorable to the plaintiffs, may be stated briefly. On November 14, 1988, Lounsbury and Donaldson were in their place of business in Madison, Connecticut, when one Deidre Adams, with whom Donaldson at one time had had a romantic relationship, entered the premises. According to plaintiffs, Adams proceeded to assault first Lounsbury and then Donaldson. During the course of the assault, Lounsbury managed to make two emergency calls to the Madison Police Department. In the interval before the arrival of the police, the assault continued and Donaldson attempted to restrain Adams.

Defendants were members of the Madison Police Department. Four of them responded to Lounsbury's complaint, characterized as an assault by a "violent female," and arrived to find Donaldson struggling with Adams on the floor. After a brief investigation, the officers arrested Lounsbury, Donaldson, and Adams, charging all three with assault.

After numerous appearances in criminal court, Lounsbury and Donaldson had the charges against them dismissed. They eventually filed the present suits, which were later consolidated, seeking damages against the officers under 42 U.S.C. § 1983 for false arrest, alleging, *inter alia,* that defendants had failed to ascertain who the complainant was. Both suits were filed in August 1991–Lounsbury's on August 7 and Donaldson's on August 20–some two years and nine months after the arrests.

Following discovery, defendants moved for summary judgment on the ground, *inter alia,* that the relevant statute of limitations for § 1983 actions is Conn.Gen.Stat. § 52–584, which provides a two-year limitations period, and that plaintiffs' suits were therefore time-barred. Plaintiffs opposed the motion, arguing that the pertinent provision is Conn.Gen.Stat. § 52–577, a three-year statute, and thus their suits were timely.

In a Ruling on Motions for Summary Judgment dated September 13, 1993 ("Ruling"), the district court granted defendants' motions for summary judgment. Although under the pertinent Supreme Court decisions the appropriate statute of limitations is the state's general or residual statute of limitations for personal injury actions, the district court concluded that Connecticut has two residual statutes of limitation for personal injury claims, one for injuries inflicted intentionally (§ 52–577), and another for injuries caused by negligent, reckless, or wanton misconduct (§ 52–584).

Ruling at 5 (emphasis added). On the premise that § 1983 was historically directed at failures to perform official duties rather than at intentional inflictions of harm, Ruling at 67, the district court concluded that § 52–584, covering personal injuries caused by negligent, reckless, or wanton conduct, is "representative of a broader range of claims typically brought under § 1983," Ruling at 6, and thus is the more appropriate statute. Since § 52584 provides a two-year limitations period, the court dismissed plaintiffs' claims, filed more than two years after their claims had accrued, as time-barred. This appeal followed.

## II. DISCUSSION

On appeal, plaintiffs renew their contention that the statute of limitations applicable to § 1983 claims in Connecticut is § 52–577, a three-year statute, rather than the two-year statute applied by the district court. We agree.

### A. *The Framework Established by the Supreme Court*

Since Congress did not enact a statute of limitations governing actions brought under § 1983, the courts must borrow a state statute of limitations. * * *. The statute to be borrowed is the one that is "most appropriate," *id.,* or "most analogous," * * * so long as it is not inconsistent with federal law or policy.

The courts' attempts to determine which statutes of limitations were most appropriate or most analogous to the various types of § 1983 claims before them, however, led to uncertainty, confusion, and lack of uniformity. * * * ("The practice of seeking state-law analogies for particular § 1983 claims bred confusion and inconsistency in the lower courts and generated time-consuming litigation."). Accordingly, in *Wilson,* recognizing that "[a]lmost every § 1983 claim can be favorably analogized to more than one of the ancient common-law forms of action, each of which may be governed by a different statute of limitations," * * * the Supreme Court concluded that the federal interests in uniformity, certainty, and the minimization of unnecessary litigation required that a single characterization of § 1983 claims be adopted. Noting that "Mlle atrocities that concerned Congress in 1871 plainly sounded in tort," * * * that "the § 1983 remedy encompasses a broad range of potential tort analogies, from injuries to property to infringements of individual liberty," * * * and that "[g]eneral personal injury actions, sounding in tort, constitute a major part of the total volume of civil litigation in the courts today, and probably did so in 1871 when § 1983 was enacted," * * * the *Wilson* Court concluded that for statute-of-limitations purposes, "§ 1983 claims are best characterized as personal injury actions," * * *. Thus a state's personal-injury statute of limitations, assuming the state has but one such statute, should be applied to all § 1983 claims.

In *Owens,* the Supreme Court dealt with the question of which statute of limitations is the appropriate one when a state has more than one personal-injury statute of limitations. Seeking to continue the simplifying process begun by the *Wilson* Court, the *Owens* Court strove to formulate "a rule for determining the appropriate personal injury limitations statute that can be applied with ease and predictability in all 50 States." * * *. The *Owens* Court observed that "[i]n marked contrast to the multiplicity of state intentional tort statutes of limitations, every State has one *general or residual* statute of limitations governing personal injury actions." * * * *Owens* described a "general provision" as one "which applies to all personal injury actions with certain specific exceptions," * * * and a "residual provision" as one "which applies to all actions not specifically provided for, including personal injury actions," * * *. The Court noted that "these provisions are easily identifiable by language or application. Indeed, the very idea of a general or residual statute suggests that each State would have no more than one." * * *.

Accordingly, in *Owens,* the Supreme Court held that if a state has more than one personal-injury statute of limitations, the state's general or residual statute of limitations for personal injury actions is to be applied: "[W]here state law provides multiple statutes of limitations for personal injury actions, courts considering § 1983 claims should borrow the general or residual statute for personal injury actions." * * *

B. *The Connecticut Statutes*

The two provisions of the Connecticut General Statutes on which the district court focused in the present case are § 52–577 and § 52–584. Section 52–577 provides:

No action founded upon a tort shall be brought but within three years from the date of the act or omission complained of.

Conn.Gen.Stat. § 52–577. Section § 52–584 provides:

No action to recover damages for injury to the person, or to real or personal property, caused by negligence, or by reckless or wanton misconduct, or by malpractice of a physician, surgeon, dentist, podiatrist, chiropractor, hospital or sanatorium, shall be brought but within two years from the date when the injury is first sustained or discovered....

Conn.Gen.Stat. § 52–584. In addition, Connecticut has other sections specifying the limitations periods covering other types of personal injury claims. *See, e.g., id. §* 52–577d (for personal injuries to minors); *id. §* 52–577c (for injuries due to hazardous chemicals); *id.* 52–577a (for product liability claims). Plainly, then, Connecticut has multiple statutes of limitations dealing with various types of claims for personal injury. Accordingly, the courts are required to apply Connecticut's general or residual personal-injury statute of limitations to claims brought under § 1983.

Contrary to the district court's conclusion, § 52–584 is not a "residual" statute as described by *Owens,* for it contains no language suggesting that it "applies to all actions not specifically provided for, including personal injury actions," * * *. Nor is § 52–584 a "general" statute, for it does not "appl[y] to all personal injury actions with certain specific exceptions," * * *. Rather, that section applies only to those actions, primarily negligence actions, that are specifically enumerated in the section itself; it does not apply to "all personal injury actions" and does not appear to reach any categories of personal injury actions that are not there enumerated.

In contrast, § 52–577, though it does not precisely follow the contours of the "general" or "residual" provisions set out in *Owens,* is a general statute of the type to which *Owens* referred. The law of torts encompasses personal injuries (as well as injuries to other personal interests) resulting from both negligent and intentional conduct, and § 52–577, by providing simply for all actions "founded upon a tort," sets the limitations period for all types of tort claims that are not specifically covered by different limitations provisions. Thus, the provision in § 52–584 for a two-year period of limitations governing personal injury actions that arise from negligence or from reckless or wanton misconduct, and the provisions in sections such as § 52–577c for a two-year period of limitations governing injuries from hazardous pollutants, merely specify exceptions to the general three-year period established in § 52–577. Unless there is such an explicit statutory provision, every tort claim governed by a Connecticut statute of limitations is subject to § 52–577's three-year period.

In sum, the pivotal question in the *Owens* analysis is what state statute of limitations applies to unenumerated personal injury claims. In Connecticut, the answer is § 52–577.

Accordingly, § 52–577 should have been applied to plaintiffs' claims under § 1983. Since § 52–577 provides a three-year period of limitations, plaintiffs' claims were not barred.

CONCLUSION

For the foregoing reasons, the judgment of the district court is reversed, and the matter is remanded for further proceedings.

## HARDIN v. STRAUB

490 U.S. 536 (1998)

JUSTICE STEVENS delivered the opinion of the Court.

This case presents the question whether a federal court applying a state statute of limitations to an inmate's federal civil rights action should give effect to the State's provision tolling the limitations period for prisoners.

Petitioner is incarcerated in a Michigan state prison. In 1986 he filed a *pro se* complaint pursuant to 42 U.S.C. § 1983, alleging that for approximately 180 days in 1980 and 1981 he had been held in solitary confinement in violation of his federal constitutional rights. The District Court *sua sponte* dismissed the complaint because it had been filed after the expiration of Michigan's 3–year statutory limitations period for personal injury actions. The Court of Appeals affirmed. * * * Following its 3–day–old decision in *Higley v. Michigan Department of Corrections,* ... the court refused to apply a Michigan statute that suspends limitations periods for persons under a legal disability until one year after the disability has been removed. Because that holding appeared to conflict with our decision in *Board of Regents, University of New York v. Tomanio,* * * * we granted certiorari. * * * We now reverse.

In enacting 42 U.S.C. § 1988 Congress determined that gaps in federal civil rights acts should be filled by state law, as long as that law is not inconsistent with federal law. See *Burnett v. Grattan,* * * *. Because no federal statute of limitations governs, federal courts routinely measure the timeliness of federal civil rights suits by state law. * * * This tradition of borrowing analogous limitations statutes, * * * is based on a congressional decision to defer to "the State's judgment on the proper balance between the policies of repose and the substantive policies of enforcement embodied in the state cause of action." *Wilson v. Garcia,** * * "In virtually all statutes of limitations the chronological length of the limitation period is interrelated with provisions regarding tolling, revival, and questions of application." *Johnson, supra,* * * *. Courts thus should not unravel state limitations rules unless their full application would defeat the goals of the federal statute at issue. See, *e.g., Wilson, supra,* * * *.

These principles were invoked in *Board of Regents, University of New York v. Tomanio, supra,* to review a contention that a § 1983 action was barred by New York's 3–year limitations statute. The District Court and the Court of Appeals had rejected the defense by relying on a "federal tolling rule" not contained among the tolling provisions the state legislature had codified with its limitations periods. *Id.,* * * *. This Court reversed. Limitations periods in § 1983 suits are to be determined by reference to the appropriate "state statute of limitations and the coordinate tolling rules"; New York's legislative choices in this regard were therefore "binding rules of law." * * * Since the State's rules did not defeat either § 1983's chief goals of compensation and deterrence or its subsidiary goals of uniformity and federalism, the Court held that Tomanio's suit was time barred. *Id.* * * *

It is undisputed that the limitations period applicable to this case is three years, as established in Michigan's statute governing personal injury actions.

See *Owens v. Okure,* * * *; *Wilson v. Garcia, supra.* Since 1846, however, the Michigan Legislature has enacted provisions tolling the onset of limitations periods for prisoners and others suffering from legal disabilities. The contemporary counterpart provides:

"[I]f the person first entitled to make an entry or bring an action is under 18 years of age, insane, or imprisoned at the time the claim accrues, the person or those claiming under the person shall have 1 year after the disability is removed through death or otherwise, to make the entry or bring the action although the period of limitations has run." Mich.Comp.Laws Ann. § 600.5851(1) (1987).

* * * The Court of Appeals for the Sixth Circuit nonetheless refused to apply the tolling provision to inmates' § 1983 suits in this case and in *Higley v. Michigan Department of Corrections,* * * *.

* * * We do not agree with the Court of Appeals. * * *

The judgment of the Court of Appeals is reversed, and the case is remanded for further proceedings consistent with this opinion.

*It is so ordered.*

## B. Relying on F.R.C.P. 15(c)(1)(C)

In sorting out the questions posed in this simulation, you should consider whether the following two cases provide any help for the Plaintiff. Specifically, do they support the Plaintiff's efforts to amend her complaint to add the new defendants?

### WORTHINGTON v. WILSON

8 F.3d 1253 (7th Cir. 1993)

MANION, CIRCUIT JUDGE.

In his 42 U.S.C. § 1983 complaint, Richard Worthington claimed that while being arrested the arresting officers purposely injured him. When he filed suit on the day the statute of limitations expired, he named "three unknown named police officers" as defendants. Worthington later sought to amend the complaint to substitute police officers Dave Wilson and Jeff Wall for the unknown officers. The district court concluded that the relation back doctrine of Fed.R.Civ.P. 15(c) did not apply, and dismissed the amended complaint. *Worthington v. Wilson,* * * *. We affirm.

I.

On February 25, 1989, Richard Worthington was arrested by a police officer in the Peoria Heights Police Department. At the time of his arrest, Worthington had an injured left hand, and he. advised the arresting officer of his injury. According to Worthington's complaint, the arresting officer responded by grabbing Worthington's injured hand and twisting it, prompting Worthington to push the officer away and tell him to "take it easy." A second police officer arrived at the scene, and Worthington was wrestled to the ground and handcuffed. The police officers then hoisted Worthington from the ground by the handcuffs, which caused him to suffer broken bones in his left hand.

Exactly two years later, on February 25, 1991, Worthington filed a five-count complaint in the Circuit Court of Peoria County, Illinois, against the Village of Peoria Heights and "three unknown named police officers," stating the above facts and alleging that he was deprived of his constitutional rights in violation of 42 U.S.C. § 1983. Counts one through three of the complaint named the police officers in their personal and official capacities, and alleged a variety of damages. Counts four and five named the Village of Peoria Heights, and alleged that it was liable for the police officers' conduct based on the doctrine of respondeat superior.

The Village removed the action to federal court and sought dismissal under Fed.R.Civ.P. 12(b)(6) for the reason that respondeat superior was not a valid basis for imposing liability against it under § 1983. At a hearing on the motion to dismiss, Worthington voluntarily dismissed his claims against the Village and obtained leave to file an amended complaint. * * *

On June 17, 1991, Worthington filed an amended complaint in which he substituted as the defendants Dave Wilson and Jeff Wall, two of the twelve or so members of the Peoria Heights Police Department, for the "unknown named police officers" who arrested him on February 25, 1989. Wilson and Wall moved to dismiss the amended complaint primarily on grounds that Illinois' two-year statute of limitations expired, Ill.Ann.Stat. ch. 735, ¶ 5/13202 (Smith—Hurd 1993), and that the amendment did not relate back to the filing of the original complaint under Rule 5(c). Worthington responded to this motion, and a hearing was conducted before a magistrate judge on October 31, 1991.

On December 19, 1991, the magistrate judge recommended that Wilson's and Wall's motion to dismiss and the Village's motion for sanctions should be granted. Worthington filed objections to these recommendations, to which the defendants responded.

On March 17, 1992, the district judge held a hearing on the objections to the magistrate judge's recommendations. Prior to the hearing, the district judge notified the parties that Rule 15(c), on which Wilson and Wall based their argument, had been amended effective December 1, 1991, and asked them to address the effect of this amendment on the motion to dismiss.

On April 27, 1992, the district judge granted Wilson's and Wall's motion to dismiss the amended complaint under revised Rule 15(c) * * *. *Worthington v. Wilson,* * * *. Worthington appeals this dismissal. * * *.

II.

Rule 15(c) was amended to provide broader "relation back" of pleadings when a plaintiff seeks to amend his complaint to change defendants. Rule 15(c) as amended December 1, 1991, provides, in pertinent part:

> An amendment of a pleading relates back to the date of the original pleading when (1) relation back is permitted by the law that provides

the statute of limitations applicable to the action, or (2) the claim or defense asserted in the amended pleading arose out of the conduct, transaction, or occurrence set forth or attempted to be set forth in the original pleadings, or (3) the amendment changes the party or the naming of the party against whom a claim is asserted if the foregoing provision (2) is satisfied and, within the period provided by Rule 4(j) for service of the summons and complaint, the party to be brought in by amendment (A) has received such notice of the institution of the action that the party will not be prejudiced in maintaining a defense on the merits, and (B) knew or should have known that, but for a mistake concerning the identity of the proper party, the action would have been brought against the party.

Prior to this amendment, the standard for relation back under Rule 15(c) was set out in *Schiavone v. Fortune,* * * *:

> The four prerequisites to a 'relation back' amendment under Rule 15(c) are: (1) the basic claim must have arisen out of the conduct set forth in the original pleading; (2) the party to be brought in must have received such notice that it will not be prejudiced in maintaining its defense; (3) that party must or should have known that, but for a mistake concerning identity, the action would have been brought against it; and (4) the second and third requirements must have been fulfilled within the proscribed limitations period.

* * *

The Advisory Committee Notes to amended Rule 15(c) indicate that the amendment repudiates the holding in *Schiavone* that notice of a lawsuit's pendency must be given within the applicable statute of limitations period. The Advisory Committee stated:

> An intended defendant who is notified of an action within the period allowed by [Rule 4(j)] for service of a summons and complaint may not under the revised rule defeat the action on account of a defect in the pleading with respect to the defendant's name, provided that the requirements of clauses (A) and (B) have been met. If the notice requirement is met within the [Rule 4(j)] period, a complaint may be amended at any time to correct a formal defect such as a misnomer or misidentification.

Fed.R.Civ.P. 15(c), Advisory Committee Notes (1991 Amendment).

In the order amending Rule 15(c), the Supreme Court expressed its intention that "insofar as just and practicable," the amendment governs cases pending in the district courts on December 1, 1991. Order Adopting Amendments to Federal Rules of Civil Procedure, 111 S.Ct. 813 (Apr. 30, 1991).

In this case, Wilson and Wall did not know of Worthington's action before the limitations period expired, as was required by *Schiavone,* but they were aware of its pendency within the extra 120 days provided by new Rule 15(c). *Worthington,* * * *. Since the amendment was decisive to the issue of "notice," the district judge retroactively applied new Rule 15(c), finding it "just and practicable" to do so. *Id.* at 833–34. We have no need to consider the retroactivity of amended Rule 15(c) as it might apply in this case because Worthington's amended complaint did not relate back under either the old or new version of Rule 15(c).

Both versions of Rule 15(c) require that the new defendants "knew or should have known that, but for a mistake concerning the identity of the proper party, the action would have been brought against the party." In *Wood v. Worachek,* * * *, we construed the "mistake" requirement of Rule 15(c):

> A plaintiff may usually amend his complaint under Rule 15(c) to change the theory or statute under which recovery is sought; or to correct a misnomer of plaintiff where the proper party plaintiff is in court; or to change the capacity in which the plaintiff sues; or to substitute or add as plaintiff the real party interest; or to add additional plaintiffs where the action, as originally brought, was a class action. Thus, amendment with relation back is generally permitted in order to correct a misnomer of a defendant where the proper defendant is already before the court and the effect is merely to correct the name under which he issued. But a new defendant cannot normally be substituted or added by amendment after the statute of limitations has run.

> Rule 15(c)(2) [current Rule 15(c)(3)] permits an amendment to relate back only where there has been an error made concerning the identity of the proper party and where that party is chargeable with knowledge of the mistake, but it does not permit relation back where, as here, there is a lack of knowledge of the proper party. Thus, in the absence of a mistake in the identification of the proper party, it is irrelevant for the purposes of Rule 15(c)(2) [current Rule 15(c)(3)] whether or not the purported substitute party knew or should have known that the action would have been brought against him. * * *

The record shows that there was no mistake concerning the identity of the police officers. At oral argument, counsel for Worthington indicated that he did not decide to file suit until one or two days before the statute of limitations had expired. At that point, neither Worthington nor his counsel knew the names of the two police officers who allegedly committed the offense. Thus, the complaint was filed against "unknown police officers." Because Worthington's failure to name Wilson and Wall was due to a lack of knowledge as to their identity, and not a mistake in their names, Worthington was prevented from availing himself of the relation back doctrine of Rule 15(c).

Worthington argues that the amended complaint should relate back based on the district judge's proposed reading of Rule 15(c) as not having a separate "mistake" requirement. The district judge construed the word "mistake" to mean "change the party or the naming of the party." Worthington, * * *. This construction, however, ignores the continuing vitality of Wood's holding which interprets the "mistake" requirement under the old version of Rule 15(c). That holding remains unaffected by the 1991 amendment to Rule 15(c). * * *

We conclude that the amendment adding Wilson and Wall failed to satisfy the "mistake" requirement of Rule 15(c). As a result, relation back was precluded, and Worthington's complaint was time-barred under Illinois law. * * *

AFFIRMED.

## SMITH v. CITY OF PHILADELPHIA, ET AL.

363 F. Supp. 2d 795 (2005)

ANITA B. BRODY, DISTRICT JUDGE.

*Pro se* plaintiff Benjamin Smith ("Smith") brings this action under 42 U.S.C. § 1983 against defendants City of Philadelphia ("the City"), Commissioner John Timoney ("Timoney"), Inspector Michael Banach ("Banach"), Captain Thomas Nestel ("Nestel"), Sergeant James Kimrey ("Kimrey") Police Officer ("P/O") Jerold Seiple ("Seiple"), P/O Nathaniel Smith ("N.Smith"), P/0 John Bender ("Bender"), and P/O Mariiza Mendez ("Mendez"). Jurisdiction is based on the existence of a federal question. Currently before me is a motion to dismiss by defendants Timoney, Banach, Nestel, Bender, and Mendez. For the reasons set forth below, the motion is granted as to defendant Timoney and denied as to defendants Banach, Nestel, Bender, and Mendez ("moving defendants").

### BACKGROUND

On September 8, 2003, plaintiff Smith filed an application to proceed *in forma pauperis*. At the same time, Smith submitted to the clerk's office his original complaint alleging racial profiling and the use of excessive force in the course of his arrest on September 7, 2001. (Compl. at 4–5.) The original complaint named as defendants the City, Seiple, N. Smith, P/0 John Doe, P/0 Jane Doe, and "Sgt. John Doe (Kimery #8696)." *(Id.* at 1.) Smith's original complaint also named the Philadelphia Police Department as a defendant.

On January 12, 2004, I granted Smith leave to proceed *in forma pauperis* and Smith's original complaint was formally filed.

On January 14, 2004, Smith filed a motion for leave to amend the complaint. I granted the motion on February 11, 2004 and the first amended complaint was officially filed on that date. The first amended complaint added defendants "Commissioner John Doe of the Philadelphia Police Department," and "Commander John Doe 24th & 25th District." (First Am. Compl. at 1.)

On March 1, 2004, Smith filed a motion to compel discovery "attempting to identify the following defendants for the required service of process: (1) Officer John and Jane Doe, operating Unit 26T4, the vehicle which transported the plaintiff to the hospital on September 7, 2001 at approx. 2:30 a.m. (2) Sgt. John Doe, supervisor at scene of arrest and the hospital. (3) Ex–Police Commissioner John Timoney and 24th and 25th Police District Commander." (Mot. Compel at 1.)

On April 7, 2004, Assistant City Solicitor Peter Han ("Han"), filed an answer to Smith's first amended complaint on behalf of defendants the City, Seiple, and N. Smith. On the same date, Han also filed a response to Smith's motion to compel on behalf of defendants the City, Seiple, and N. Smith.

Exhibit C of defendants' response was the "Answers and Objections of [defendants] to Plaintiff's First Set of Interrogatories." (Defs.' Resp. Opp'n Pl.'s Mot. Compel Ex. C.) Exhibit C identified Bender and Mendez as the officers who transported plaintiff to the hospital on September 7, 2001. *(Id.* at 2.) Exhibit C also identified Banach and Nestel as the commanders of the 24th and 25th Districts. *(Id.)*

On July 8, 2004, Smith filed a motion for leave to amend his complaint. I granted that motion on July 13, 2004, and Smith's second amended complaint was filed on that day. The second amended complaint named as defendants the City, Timoney, Banach, Nestel, Kimrey, Seiple, N. Smith, Bender and Mendez. (Second Am. Compl. at 1.)

On August 27, 2004, Assistant City Soliciter Han filed an answer to plaintiff's second amended complaint on behalf of defendants the City, Seiple, N. Smith, and Kimrey. Also on August 27, 2004, Han filed the instant motion to dismiss on behalf of moving defendants.

* * *

**DISCUSSION**

Moving defendants argue that Smith's claims against them should be dismissed because the claims were made after the statute of limitations had run. (Mot. Dismiss at 4.) The statute of limitations for Smith's claims ran on September 8, 2003. Smith did not individually name the moving defendants in this lawsuit until he filed his second amended complaint on July 13, 2004, after the statute of limitations had run.

Smith argues that his second amended complaint relates back to the date of his original complaint under Federal Rule of Civil Procedure 15(c)(3), allowing for relation back of amendments that change parties or add new parties. Therefore, Smith argues, his claims against moving defendants were filed within the statute of limitations. (Pl.'s Opp'n Mot. Dismiss at 1.) For the reasons set forth below, Smith's claims against the moving defendants satisfy the requirements for relation back under Rule 15(c)(3).

Rule 15(c) provides:

(c) Relation Back of Amendments. An amendment of a pleading relates back to the date of the original pleading when

(1) relation back is permitted by the law that provides the statute of limitations applicable to the action, or

(2) the claim or defense asserted in the amended pleading arose out of the conduct, transaction, or occurrence set forth or attempted to be set forth in the original pleading, or

(3) the amendment changes the party or the naming of the party against whom a claim is asserted if the foregoing provision (2) is satisfied and, within the period provided by Rule 4(m) for service of the summons and complaint, the party to be brought in by amendment (A) has received such notice of the institution of the action that the party will not be prejudiced in maintaining

a defense on the merits, and (B) knew or should have known that, but for a mistake concerning the identity of the proper party, the action would have been brought against the party.[3]

F.R.Civ. P. 15(c). Because Smith's second amended complaint both added new defendants and changed originally named defendants subsection (3) of the Rule is applicable. In order for Smith's second amended complaint to relate back to the date of his original complaint under Rule 15(c)(3), three conditions must be met. First, Smith's claims against the moving defendants must arise "out of the conduct, transaction, or occurrence set forth or attempted to be set forth in the original pleading." Second, within 120 days of the filing of Smith's original complaint, the moving defendants must have "received such notice of the action that [they] will not be prejudiced in maintaining a defense on the merits." The Third Circuit has interpreted the second requirement as prongs, notice and the absence of prejudice, each of which must be satisfied. Third, it must be that within 120 days of the filing of Smith's original complaint, the moving defendants "knew or should have known that, but for a mistake concerning the identity of the proper party, the action would have been brought against [the moving defendants]." * * *

*Claims arose out of the same conduct*

The parties do not dispute that Smith meets the first requirement for relation back: that his claims against moving defendants arose from the same conduct as that alleged in his original complaint. Smith's allegations against the moving defendants in his second amended complaint arose out of his arrest on September 7, 2001, the same occurrence that he set forth in his original pleading. (Compl. at 4; Second Am. Compl. at 1.) Therefore, the first requirement is satisfied.

*Notice*

The first prong of the second requirement for relation back requires that moving defendants received, within 120 days of the filing of the original complaint, notice of Smith's action. One hundred and twenty days from the official filing of Smith's complaint was May 11, 2004. In the Third Circuit, notice can be actual or constructive. * * *. Constructive notice is possible through the "shared attorney" method or through the "identity of interest" method. * * * Smith does not argue that the moving defendants received actual notice of his action by May 11, 2004. Rather, Smith argues that the moving defendants received notice of his action through both the shared attorney method and the imputed interest method. (Pl.'s Opp'n Mot. Dismiss at 3–4.)

In analyzing the shared attorney method, "the relative inquiry ... is whether notice of the institution of this action can be imputed to the defendant sought to be named within the relevant 120 day period ... by virtue of representation he shared with a defendant originally named in the lawsuit." * * * The "fundamental issue here is whether the attorney's later relationship with the newly named defendant gives rise to the inference that the

3. Editor's note: The F.R.C.P. were "restyled," effective December 1, 2007. The changes in the language of the rules were not intended to change their meaning.

attorney, *within the 120 day period, had some communication or relationship with, and thus gave notice of the action to, the newly named defendant.*" * * *.

The record in this case shows that moving defendants share the same attorney as the original defendants. All current defendants were represented by the same attorney-Assistant City Solicitor Peter Han. The record also shows that prior to May 11, 2004, there was some communication or relationship between the attorney for the original defendants and four of the five newly-named defendants. On March 1, 2004, Smith filed a motion to compel discovery seeking the identity of the John and Jane Does named in his original complaint and his first amended complaint. (Mot. to Compel at 1; Compl. at 1; First Am. Compl. at 1.) Han's April 7, 2004 response to Smith's discovery motion identified defendants Bender and Mendez as the officers who transported Smith to and from the hospital on the night of his arrest. (Defs.' Resp. Opp'n Pl.'s Mot. Compel Ex. C.) The response also identified Banach and Nestel as the commanders of the 24th and 25th police districts. *(Id.)* Han's response to Smith's discovery motion indicates that the relationship between Han and defendants Bender, Mendez, Banach and Nestel existed at least as of April 7, 2004, well within the 120–day period. Therefore, through the shared attorney method, notice of Smith's action may be imputed to defendants Bender, Mendez, Banach and Nestel. Defendant Timoney was not named in Defs' Resp. Opp'n Pl.'s Mot. Compel Ex. C. Without other evidence of some communication or relationship between Han and Timoney within the 120–day period, notice of Smith's action may not be imputed to Timoney through the shared attorney method. * * *

In *Garvin,* the Third Circuit examined and rejected a plaintiffs shared attorney argument due to insufficient evidence of shared representation. * * * The plaintiff in *Garvin* attempted to amend her original complaint against the City and John Doe by substituting four individually named officers for one John Doe named in her original complaint. * * * The district court denied her motion to amend, finding that it was filed after the statute of limitations had passed, that plaintiff did not meet the requirements for relation back under Rule 15(c)(3), and that therefore the amendment would be futile because the amended complaint could not have withstood a motion to dismiss on the basis of the statute of limitations. * * *The Third Circuit affirmed the district court. * * *

In rejecting plaintiffs shared attorney argument, the Third Circuit in *Garvin* focused on the fact that plaintiff failed to "come forth with evidence that gives rise to the inference that Deputy City Solicitor Sitarski [attorney for the City] or anyone else in the City Solicitor's office had any communication or relationship whatsoever with the four officers within the 120–day period so as to justify imputing notice to the officers." * * * In order to avail him or herself of the shared attorney method of imputing notice, "a plaintiff must show 'some communication or relationship' between the shared attorney and the John Doe defendant prior to the expiration of the 120–day period." * * *. The court also noted that the "four newly named defendants were not and are not currently represented by the City's attorney." * * *

Unlike *Garvin,* the record in Smith's case shows that there was some communication or relationship between the attorney for the original defendants, Assistant City Solicitor Han, and the moving defendants. First, all defendants are currently represented by the same attorney, the City Solicitor's office. More importantly, before Smith filed his second amended complaint, Han filed a response to Smith's discovery motion identifying moving defendants as the John and Jane Doe parties named in plaintiffs original complaint and first amended complaint. (Defs.' Resp. Opp'n Pl.'s Mot. Compel Ex. C.) This response was filed on April 7, 2004, over a month prior to the expiration of the 120–day period on May 11, 2004. Han's response provides the evidence that the Third Circuit found to be missing in *Garvin*. Han's response gives rise to the inference that the attorney for the original defendants, "within the 120 day period, had some communication or relationship with, and thus gave notice of the action to, the newly named defendant." * * * Therefore, notice of Smith's action may be imputed to defendants Bender, Mendez, Banach and Nestel through the shared attorney method.

Smith also argues that notice to defendants Banach and Nestel may be imputed through the identity of interest method. (Pl.'s Opp'n Mot. Dismiss at 4.) Under the identity of interest method, courts in the Third Circuit "also will impute notice if the parties are so closely related in their business operations or other activities that filing suit against one serves to provide notice to the other of the pending litigation." * * * In *Garvin* and *Singletary,* the Third Circuit held that "a non-management employee … does not share a sufficient nexus of interests with his or her employer so that notice given to the employer can be imputed to the employee for Rule 15(c)(3) purposes." * * *. Unlike the newly named defendants in *Garvin* and *Singletary,* defendants Banach, commander of the 24th police district, and Nestel, commander of the 25th police district, hold supervisory positions in the Philadelphia Police Department, an originally-named defendant. In their supervisory positions, defendants Banach and Nestel share a sufficient nexus of interest with their employer that notice to the police department of Smith's lawsuit can be imputed to defendants Banach and Nestel. Therefore, notice to defendants Banach and Nestel may also be imputed through the identity of interest method.

Smith also argues that defendant Timoney received notice through the identity of interest method. (Pl.'s Opp'n Mot. Dismiss at 4.) I take judicial notice of the fact that Timoney was no longer Police Commissioner at the time Smith's suit was filed. Because Timoney was no longer a supervisory employee of the Philadelphia Police Department at the time the suit was filed, he did not share an identity of interest with the police department at that time and notice cannot be imputed to him in this manner.

The record does not show whether defendants Banach and Nestle held their positions as commanders of the 24th and 25th police districts at the time Smith's suit was filed. Because this is a motion to dismiss, I accept as true the factual allegations in the complaint and all reasonable inferences that can be drawn therefrom. For purposes of the instant motion, I assume Banach and Nestel held supervisory positions at the time Smith's suit was filed and that notice maybe imputed to them through the identity of interest method. However, even if Banach and Nestel did not receive constructive notice through the identity of interest method, they did receive constructive notice through the shared attorney method. *See supra* pp. 7–10.

*Absence of prejudice*

The second prong of the second requirement for relation back under Rule 15(c)(3) is a prejudice inquiry that focuses on whether a newly-named defendant is "one who, for lack of timely notice that a suit has been instituted, must set about assembling evidence and constructing a defense when the case is already stale." * * *. Smith's second amended complaint alleges injuries arising from the same incident, his arrest of September 7, 2001, as that described in his original complaint. Smith's claims against moving defendants are similar to the claims he made against the original defendants. The overlapping claims contained in both the original and the second amended complaint include excessive use of force; failure to properly train, supervise, and discipline police officers, and police coverup. (Compl. at 4–5; Second Am. Compl. at 1–3.) Because Smith's claims in the second amended complaint are essentially unchanged from the claims in his original complaint, the evidence relevant to a defense against these claims are similar for both the moving defendants' and the original defendants. Additionally, because moving defendants share the same counsel as the originally named defendants, moving defendants' counsel had access to all evidence regarding the allegations in the second amended complaint in a timely fashion. Therefore, moving defendants have not been prejudiced in assembling evidence or constructing a defense. * * *. Smith satisfies the second prong of the second requirement for relation back under Rule 15(c)(3) because there is no indication that the moving defendants have been prejudiced in maintaining a defense on the merits.

Because moving defendants received constructive notice of Smith's action, either through the shared attorney method or the identity of interest method, within 120 days of the filing of Smith's original complaint, and because the notice was sufficient such that moving defendants will not be prejudiced in maintaining a defense on merits, Smith's second amended complaint satisfies the second requirement of Rule 15(c)(3) for relation back to the date of his original complaint.

*"But for a mistake"*

Rule 15(c)(3)(B) provides the third and final requirement for relation back: it must be that within 120 days of the filing of Smith's original complaint, the moving defendants knew or should have known that, but for a mistake concerning the identity of the proper party, the action would have been brought against them. In the Third Circuit "the amendment of a 'John Doe' complaint [can meet] all of the conditions for Rule 15(c)(3) relations back, including the 'but for a mistake' requirement." * * *. As noted above, the moving defendants in Smith's second amended complaint received notice of the action within 120 days of the filing of Smith's original complaint. Smith's original complaint identified P/Os John and Jane Doe as being present during the incident of September 7, 2001. (Compl. at 1, 4–5.) Smith then filed a discovery motion seeking the identity of P/Os John and Jane Doe. (Mot.Compel.) On April 7, 2004, in response to Smith's discovery motion, counsel for the defendants identified Bender and Mendez as "Officer John and Jane Doe, operating Unit 26T4, the vehicle which transported the plaintiff to the hospital on September 7, 2001 at approx. 2:30 a.m." Given that counsel for Bender and Mendez identified Bender and Mendez as P/Os John and Jane Doe in Smith's complaint, Bender and Mendez knew or should have know that Smith would have named them in his complaint if he had known their names. As for defendants Banach and Nestel, Smith's first amended complaint added "Commander John Doe 24th and 25th District" as defendants. On April 7, 2004, counsel for the moving defendants filed an answer to this complaint. Moving defendants Banach and Nestel, who held the positions of Commanders of the 24th and 25th police districts, knew or should have known that Smith would have named them individually in this action had he known their names. Therefore, as to all four moving defendants, Smith's second amended complaint satisfies the third and final requirement for relation back under Rule 15(c)(3).

## CONCLUSION

For the reasons stated above, Smith's second amended complaint against the moving defendants satisfies all the requirements for relation back to the date of his original complaint under Rule 15(c)(3). Therefore, Smith's claims against the moving defendants were made within the statute of limitations, and the motion to dismiss is denied as to defendants Banach, Nestel, Bender and Mendez. The motion to dismiss is granted as to defendant Timoney.

# CHAPTER NINE

# MOTION TO DISMISS FOR SUMMARY JUDGMENT

## I. INTRODUCTION

Chapter Two discussed briefly the options available to a defendant upon receiving a summons and complaint. Chapters Six and Seven introduced you to some of the policy choices made by the drafters of the F.R.C.P. Specially, instead of using pleading as a way to dismiss cases unlikely to prevail on the merits, the drafters of the rules favored allowing liberal discovery. After the parties have had a full and fair opportunity to develop factual support for their claims, the rules allow a party to challenge the sufficiency of its opponents' case by bringing a motion for summary judgment. Only if a party survives that motion should the case go to trial on the merits. Thus, the rules anticipated an important role for summary judgment motions.

This chapter introduces you to this important procedural device. After a brief background discussion of summary judgment practice, this chapter presents you with three summary judgment simulation exercises. In the first, Ms. Nobile has deposed Mr. Ridge and has now completed discovery. He has denied conduct alleged in her complaint and now moves for summary judgment. The first simulation exercise requires you to consider whether the defendant has met his Rule 56(c) burden. The second simulation asks you to assume that he has met his burden and focuses on whether Ms. Nobile can resist summary judgment by claiming a right to cross-examine Mr. Ridge at trial. In the third simulation, instead of claiming only a right of cross-examination, Ms. Nobile has attached some evidence to support her claim that Mr. Ridge conspired with others to violate her rights. There, you must assess whether Ms. Nobile has provided enough evidence to meet her burden under F.R.C.P. 56(e).

## II. SUMMARY JUDGMENT MOTIONS: SOME BACKGROUND

Trials are expensive for litigants and for the system. Our court system should be open to litigants if their dispute presents genuine issues of material facts. If not, the litigant who fails to demonstrate the existence of such a factual dispute should not be entitled to a day in court. Summary judgment is the vehicle to test whether such a factual dispute exists.

Three subsections of F.R.C.P. 56 are particularly important for your understanding of summary judgment practice. F.R.C.P. 56(a) provides that the "court shall grant summary judgment if the movant shows that there is no genuine dispute as to any material fact and the movant is entitled to judgment as a matter of law." F.R.C.P. 56(c) states the burden on the moving party: s/he must cite material in the record showing that a fact cannot be genuinely disputed or must show "that the materials cited do not establish the absence or presence of a genuine dispute, or that an adverse party cannot produce admissible evidence to support the fact." This language is relatively new and replaces the traditional formulation, which stated that a party had to show "there is no genuine issue as to any material fact and ... the movant is entitled to a judgment as a matter of law." Despite the change in the language, the intent of the rule is the same. The amended language may help clarify some confusion caused by the earlier formulation and not greatly clarified by the Court's decision in *Celotex Corp. v. Catrett,* 477 U.S. 317 (1986).

If a moving party satisfies her burden under F.R.C.P. 56(c), the burden of demonstrating the existence of a genuine issue of material fact shifts to the party resisting summary judgment. The original language of F.R.C.P. 56(e) stated, in relevant part, that "When a motion for summary judgment is made and supported as provided in this rule, an adverse party may not rest upon the mere allegations or denials of the adverse party's pleading, but the adverse party's response, by affidavits or as otherwise provided in this rule, must set forth specific facts showing that there is a genuine issue for trial." The restyled F.R.C.P. 56(e) is less clear, but again, does not intend to change the responding party's burden. That party must "properly support an assertion of fact" and otherwise address the moving party's assertions of facts. Failing that, the court should enter a summary judgment if the moving party shows it is entitled to the judgment.

The rule is deceptively straightforward. Confusion has arisen surrounding a number of its terms.

The concept of materiality is easy enough. The parties may disagree about the existence of any number of facts, but disagreements that count deal only with "material" facts. Facts are material if they relate to elements of a party's claim or defense.[1] Thus, in a products liability case, the defendant may contend that its employees were not aware of the product's defect. If the governing law makes the defendant strictly liable, the parties' disagreement about the defendant's employees' knowledge is immaterial. But more complex issues arise with regard to how a party shows the absence of the dispute about material facts.

Two Supreme Court cases demonstrate the point. *Adickes v. S.H. Kress & Co.,* 398 U.S. 144 (1970), and *Celotex* involved a moving party that did not have the trial burden of proof concerning the material element they claimed was lacking. At trial, a party who does not have to prove an element of a claim can prevail by doing nothing or by getting the fact-finder to discredit its oppo-

---

1. Or as one commentator has stated, "... a material fact is one which will affect the outcome of the case...."

nent's evidence. It does not have to disprove its opponent's case. To get a summary judgment, one might ask, does the moving party have to do more than it would have to do at trial?

In *Adickes,* the defendant denied a white woman service at its lunch counter. The plaintiff had accompanied a group of African–American students to the defendant's store in Mississippi. After she left the store, a police officer arrested her for loitering. The plaintiff brought an action claiming a violation of her civil rights. To prevail on that claim, the plaintiff had to show that the defendant conspired with the state actor. Her complaint alleged that a conspiracy existed between the store employees and the officer who arrested her. It also alleged his presence in the store at the time of the incident. Seeking a summary judgment, the defendant attached affidavits of the store manager, the police chief and the arresting officer, denying any communication between the officer and the store manager. Concededly, her response did not meet her burden under F.R.C.P. 56(e). Hence, the Court had to decide whether the defendant had met its F.R.C.P. 56(c) burden.

The Court held that the district court erred in granting a summary judgment. The defendant failed to produce evidence that foreclosed the possibility that some store employee and the police officer had reached an agreement to refuse service to the plaintiff. As developed below, the Court's holding in *Celotex* is hard to reconcile with *Adickes*. But, depending on how one reads the opinion in *Adickes*, reconciling the cases is possible. Despite that, for many years, lower courts resisted granting summary judgments in reliance on broad language in *Adickes*. The Court's opinion suggested that the defendant failed to disprove the plaintiff's case. That conclusion seems inconsistent with the defendant's burden at trial, where it can force the plaintiff to prove her case and where it has to prove nothing at all.

One reason why lower courts may have been so willing to pick up on the broad language in *Adickes* is that many judges disfavor granting summary judgments. Given a commitment to providing litigants access to court, some judges are hesitant to deny a plaintiff her day in court. But such a position is also inconsistent with the role of summary judgments in weeding out nonmeritorious cases. And as indicated above, forcing a moving party to disprove her opponent's case is inconsistent with what should happen at trial.

Decided at a time when federal judges were concerned about their crowded dockets, *Celotex* signaled the Court's support for the granting of more summary judgments.[2] In *Celotex*, the plaintiff had to prove that her husband, who died of expose to asbestos, had been exposed to the defendant's product. During discovery, the plaintiff had failed to respond to an interrogatory seeking information about how the plaintiff was going to prove that element of her claim. Instead of filing a motion to compel her response to the interrogatory, the defendant moved for summary judgment. The trial court granted the motion, but the court of appeals reversed in reliance on *Adickes*. The Supreme Court's opinion is a hard read for students first exposed to summary judgment practice.

---

**2.** Empirical data suggest that the Court's decision had only a limited effect in frequency of summary judgments.

The majority reversed the appellate court's holding. Much of the discussion focuses narrowly on the language of F.R.C.P. 56 and discusses whether a moving party must attach evidence supporting its motion. But the case has a broader meaning.

*Celotex* establishes that a moving party that does not have the trial burden of persuasion does not have to negate its opponent's case in order to satisfy its F.R.C.P. 56(c) burden. That is important in a case like *Celotex*, where the defendant would have almost no chance of disproving that the decedent had ever been exposed to its product. Because it could prevail at trial if the plaintiff lacked proof of exposure, it ought to be able to test the strength of the plaintiff's case at the summary judgment stage.

An issue not resolved by the majority was how much the moving party must do. Close examination of Justice White's concurring opinion is critical. He provided the fifth vote for the lead opinion. He shared dissenting Justice Brennan's concern: a defendant like Celotex must do something more than merely state "the plaintiff cannot prove this element of her claim." Finding such a conclusory statement sufficient would allow the moving party to test the strength of its opponent's case without any meaningful reason to believe it has a chance of success. Further, it could smoke out its opponent's trial strategy at an early stage in the proceedings. As Justice White stated, "It is not enough to move for summary judgment without supporting the motion in any way or with a conclusory assertion that the plaintiff has no evidence to prove his case."

Justice White's opinion begs a question: what must the moving party do in a case like *Celotex*? Justice Brennan's dissenting opinion offers insight. There, Justice Brennan suggested that the moving party has two options. It can disprove its opponent's case. For example, if a party has a witness who can testify that the light was green in favor of a defendant involved in an intersectional collision, introducing an affidavit to that effect may directly disprove the plaintiff's allegation that the defendant ran a red light. But where a party is not in a position to disprove its opponent's case, the litigant should show the court why, based on the record, it believes that its opponent cannot prevail.[3] The Court has not returned to the issue, but following Justice Brennan's dissent is a matter of good practice.[4]

Another case decided in 1986 also demonstrates the complexity of F.R.C.P. 56. *Anderson v. Liberty Lobby, Inc.*, 477 U.S. 242 (1986), involved a story published by a magazine run by columnist Jack Anderson. The article portrayed Willis Carto and the organization he headed as neo-Nazi, anti-Semitic, racist and fascist. The plaintiffs brought a defamation action against the defendants. Upon completion of discovery, the defendants moved for summary judgment. Attached to the motion was an affidavit prepared by the employee who had written the articles at issue in the litigation. The affidavit

---

**3.** Had the defendant done so in *Celotex*, the court should have realized that the case involved a discovery dispute where the defendant should have moved to compel an answer to its interrogatories, rather than seeking a summary judgment.

**4.** Many practice guides advise compliance with Justice Brennan's dissent. Complying with Justice Brennan's dissent should always satisfy the minimum required under the rule.

set out the work that he had done, the sources that he consulted, and a statement of his own belief in the accuracy of the stories. The plaintiffs responded by pointing to claimed inaccuracies in the stories. Because Carto was a public figure, the plaintiffs had to show actual malice. The plaintiffs attempted to do so by pointing to an earlier libel suit brought by the plaintiff that resulted in a favorable settlement against Time Magazine. The plaintiffs also stated one of the authors of the Time article was an editor for the defendant-magazine. The plaintiffs also alleged that the author of the articles before the court had not met one of his sources, nor asked for that person's sources. They also showed that an editor at the magazine told Jack Anderson that the articles were terrible and ridiculous.

*Anderson* addressed three distinct legal issues. Many students focus on the most obvious aspect of the case. At trial, the plaintiffs in a libel case involving public figures must prove actual malice by clear and convincing evidence. In *Anderson*, the trial court granted the summary judgment but the court of appeals reversed. It did so because it believed the lower court should ignore the heightened burden that the plaintiffs would have to meet at trial. The Supreme Court disagreed and concluded that, "... the judge must view the evidence presented through the prism of the substantive evidentiary burden." Were that the only question resolved in *Anderson,* its precedential value would have been limited.

More importantly, the Court also discussed the standard for granting summary judgments generally. As indicated above, the plaintiffs did present some evidence supporting a finding that the defendants acted with actual malice. Earlier Supreme Court cases had held that, after trial in ruling on a motion as a matter of law, a court must apply a substantial evidence test. Such a standard is higher than a mere scintilla of evidence test. *Anderson*, in effect, created symmetry between the post-trial and pre-trial standard and held that the trial court should apply a substantial evidence test.[5] Thus, the plaintiffs in *Anderson* could not resist a summary judgment merely by showing that they produced a scintilla of evidence; they had to show that reasonable jurors could find for them based on the evidence presented.

Finally, *Anderson* addressed a third question that has caused some confusion among lower courts. What happens if a non-moving party seeks to resist summary judgment based on a right to cross-examine the opposing party or key witness at trial? In *Anderson*, the plaintiffs argued that they should be able to resist summary judgment based on the need to cross-examine the defendants at trial. The Court rejected the plaintiffs' claim.

This simulation allows you to explore many of the issues raised above. In considering whether litigant may resist summary judgment based on the right to cross-examine witnesses at trial, you must resolve who has the burden of persuasion at trial.

---

**5.** The Court's decision is not without problems and critics. As the Court observed, the trial judge is not to weigh the evidence. At the same time, applying the substantial evidence test requires an assessment of the caliber and quantity of proof available. Reconciling those two obligations seems difficult at best.

# III. THE SIMULATION

## A. Satisfying F.R.C.P. 56(c)

This simulation consists of three parts. The first part requires you to explore whether Mr. Ridge has met his F.R.C.P. 56(c) burden. Reexamine the complaint in Chapter 4. Assume that the defendants successfully removed the action to the United States District Court for the District of Connecticut. This section includes Mr. Ridge's motion for a partial summary judgment; thereafter, it includes instructions for this exercise.

In the United States District Court

for the

District of Connecticut

| | | |
|---|---|---|
| Sarah D. Nobile,<br>Plaintiff<br>v.<br>Department of Police for<br>The City of Doddville;<br>MDC, Inc.; Nathan Loewe;<br>Michael Ridge; and<br>Unnamed Officers of<br>The DPCCD;<br>Defendants | )<br>)<br>)<br>)<br>)<br>)<br>)<br>)<br>)<br>) | No. 00–34–1689 |

**MOTION FOR PARTIAL SUMMARY JUDGMENT**

Pursuant to Rule 56, Defendant Michael Ridge moves the Court for a summary judgment dismissing with prejudice Count Two of Plaintiff's Complaint, on the grounds that all of the papers on file in this case establish that no genuine issue of material fact exists and that Defendant Ridge is entitled to judgment as a matter of law.

As developed more fully in the following **Memorandum of Points and Authorities in Support of Defendant Michael Ridge's Motion for Partial Summary Judgment:**

With regard to Count Two, the evidence in the record demonstrates that Defendant Ridge did not engage in a conspiracy with any of the named co-defendants or with any unnamed persons, whereby he violated or attempted to violate the Plaintiff's right to privacy.

Wherefore, Defendant Michael Ridge asks this Court to dismiss Count Two with prejudice.

Respectfully submitted,

*R. Cooper Russell*

R. Cooper Russell
Russell and Scott
Attorneys at Law
Suite 6
McGeorge Towers
Cuomo City, New York 11774
(561) 782–0099

Attorney for Defendant Michael Ridge

Dated: November 20, YR-00

In the United States District Court

for the

District of Connecticut

| | | |
|---|---|---|
| Sarah D. Nobile, | ) | |
| Plaintiff | ) | No. 00–34–1689 |
| v. | ) | |
| Department of Police for | ) | |
| The City of Doddville; | ) | |
| MDC, Inc.; Nathan Loewe; | ) | |
| Michael Ridge; and | ) | |
| Unnamed Officers of | ) | |
| The DPCCD; | ) | |
| Defendants | ) | |

**MEMORANDUM OF POINTS AND AUTHORITIES IN SUPPORT OF DEFENDANT MICHAEL RIDGE'S MOTION FOR PARTIAL SUMMARY JUDGMENT**

1. Plaintiff has alleged in her complaint that Defendant Michael Ridge conspired to violate her right to privacy.

2. During the course of discovery, she has been able to bring forth no evidence of such a conspiracy.

3. At trial, she bears the burden of proving the existence of such a conspiracy.

4. Attached below is the relevant excerpt from Plaintiff's Deposition of Defendant Michael Ridge. The excerpt contains all of the evidence that Plaintiff has relating to whether Defendant Michael Ridge engaged in the alleged conspiracy. It conclusively proves that he did not so conspire.

5. As a result, this Court should grant Defendant Michael Ridge's Motion for Partial Summary Judgment and dismiss Count Two with prejudice.

Respectfully submitted,

*R. Cooper Russell*

R. Cooper Russell
Russell and Scott
Attorneys at Law
Suite 6
McGeorge Towers
Cuomo City, New York 11774
(561) 782–0099

Attorney for Defendant Michael Ridge

Dated: November 20, YR-00

## CERTIFICATE OF SERVICE

I hereby certify that on November 20, YR-00, I caused the following document:

DEFENDANT RIDGE'S MOTION FOR PARTIAL SUMMARY JUDGMENT

to be served on the plaintiff and plaintiff's counsel, Adrian Connell, by first class mail, postage paid.

Dated: November 20, YR-00

Respectfully submitted,

*R. Cooper Russell*

R. Cooper Russell
Russell and Scott
Attorneys at Law
Suite 6
McGeorge Towers
Cuomo City, New York 11774
(561) 782–0099

Attorney for Defendant Michael Ridge

The following excerpt is from Ridge's deposition and is the evidence that he has attached to his motion, which he claims is sufficient to meet his burden under F.R.C.P. 56(c):

Deposition of Michael Ridge

Taken by Plaintiff, at 139 McGeorge Avenue, Cuomo City, New York 11774, beginning at 9:30 A.M., October 1, YR-00, before Danielle Webster, Certified Stenographic Reporter.

Appearances:

For Plaintiff: Adrian Connell, 139 McGeorge Avenue, Cuomo City, New York 11774, Telephone: (561) 782–1897.

For Defendant: R. Cooper Russell, Russell and Scott, Attorneys at Law, Suite 6, McGeorge Towers, Cuomo City, New York 11774; Telephone: (561) 782–0099.

* * *

MS. CONNELL: Mr. Ridge, let me turn now to events directly relating to your acquisition of information allegedly linking Ms. Nobile to child pornography. And before I ask my next question, I want to remind you that Magistrate Judge Levine ruled against you and held that you do not have a right to withhold names of your sources.[6] You do understand that, don't you?

6. If you did the simulation in the Discovery chapter, you or your opponent may have argued that Ridge did not have to reveal the names of his sources. For purposes of this simulation,

A. Yes.

Q. Now, let me ask you then, you received information suggesting that Ms. Nobile's computer was the subject of a police search of Judge Elliot's chambers, isn't that correct?

A. Yes, it is.

Q. Would you please tell us how you obtained that information?

A. I received an anonymous and very detailed note containing that information.

Q. You have no idea from whom?

A. That's right.

Q. Mr. Ridge, with all due respect, if you did not know the name of the source of this information, why did you resist disclosing his or her name during discovery?

A. That was a matter of principle. I don't think anyone has the right to force a journalist to reveal his sources.

Q. So you were willing to spend time and money to establish that point even though you had no source for this story?

A. Yes.

Q. You were willing to waste the court's time and my time as well?

MR. RUSSELL: Objection. Adrian, you are arguing with Mr. Ridge.

MS. CONNELL: Mr. Russell, you know that is not the case. Let's not waste time.

MR. RUSSELL: Let's take a five minute break.

MS. CONNELL: I would rather not; this is going to be a long day and I don't want to exceed the time limits set by Rule 30.

MR. RUSSELL: Well, we will let you go over the time limits if it gets to that. We need a break.

MS. CONNELL: Okay; five minutes.

(Resuming the deposition):

MS. CONNELL: So you said you got the tip about the police search from an anonymous source, is that correct?

A. Yes.

Q. Did you attempt to confirm its accuracy or were you going to publish that information without checking your sources?

A. Oh, no. I did some checking.

---

assume that Ridge did resist disclosing names of his sources and that the magistrate judge ruled against him on that question.

Q. With whom?

A. John Kenworth is a sergeant on the police force.

Q. Did you ask him to reveal information about the search?

A. Not exactly.

Q. Why not?

A. He would not have told me.

Q. Then how did he confirm the story?

A. It is not that hard to get people to confirm information even when they are obligated to keep it private.

Q. How do you manage that?

A. Well, I know Kenworth. I called him and met him for coffee. I had a pretty good idea what must have happened during the police raid of Judge Elliot's chambers and so I laid out the story and watched his reaction. His face told me that the story was true.

Q. So you are telling me that you did not approach anyone in the police department to get the information originally?

A. That is right.

Q. And you did not approach anyone who worked for Judge Elliot to get the information?

A. That is right.

Q. Did you have any other sources or check with anyone else concerning the police search of Judge Elliot's chambers?

A. No, absolutely no one. * * *[7]

BY MR. RUSSELL: Just let me ask you one or two questions before we wrap up. Mr. Ridge, did you conspire with anyone to violate Ms. Nobile's right to privacy?

A. Absolutely not.

Q. Other than checking sources like you testified to earlier, did you talk to anyone about Ms. Nobile's involvement in child pornography?

A. No. Well, I did talk to the Judge's secretary.

Q. What did you discuss with her?

A. I told her what I know and waited to hear her reaction. That always tells me if I have my information right.

Q. So, to repeat, did you ever conspire to violate the plaintiff's rights?

A. No.

---

7. The deposition turned to other topics at this point, but they are not relevant to the matter before the court at this point.

* * * (At 4:45 P.M., October 1, YR-00, deposition of Michael Ridge was adjourned).

Instructions: Your professor will assign students to represent either Nobile or Ridge. S/he may have you argue the simulation orally before a magistrate judge or have you submit a brief memo discussing whether the court should grant Ridge's motion. The simulation focuses on the Court's decisions in *Adickes* and *Celotex*, discussed above: has the defendant put into the record enough evidence to switch the burden to the plaintiff?

## B. Satisfying F.R.C.P. 56(e)

The second part of this simulation focuses on whether a right to cross-examine is sufficient to resist a motion for summary judgment. In this case, counsel for the Plaintiff may question whether the Defendant's evidence satisfies his F.R.C.P. 56(c) burden. If the court finds that the Defendant's motion is insufficient, the Plaintiff's failure to respond would not matter. But failing to respond is risky. If the court finds that the Defendant's papers show the absence of a genuine issue of material fact and the Plaintiff failed to respond, the court should grant the motion. As a result, Ms. Connell plans to respond to the Defendant's motion.

For purposes of this simulation, your professor will assign you one of two roles. S/he may have you take the role of an associate in Ms. Connell's firm. Ms. Connell has asked you to prepare a short memo or oral presentation explaining whether she can resist the Defendant's motion by claiming a right to cross-examine Mr. Ridge at trial. Alternatively, s/he may assign the role of an associate for Mr. Russell and ask you whether Ms. Connell's claim that the right to cross-examine Mr. Ridge satisfies Ms. Nobile's F.R.C.P. 56(e) burden. To resolve the issue, you will need to review the three cases that you will find at the end of this chapter. In assessing those cases, you should figure out who has the trial burden of proof. That is fairly obvious in *Dyer* and *Cross*. It is harder in *Lundeen*. There, once Wife 1 puts the policy into evidence, the burden shifts to Wife 2 to show the change in beneficiaries.

## C. More on Satisfying F.R.C.P. 56(e)

The third part of this simulation is designed to test your understanding of *Anderson*. Assume that counsel for the Plaintiff has decided not to rely solely on a right to cross-examine Mr. Ridge as her basis for resisting summary judgment. Instead, she attaches the following material from Mr. Ridge's deposition and claims that this satisfies her F.R.C.P. 56(e) burden (along with her claim that she should be able to cross-examine Mr. Ridge in front of the fact-finder).

As with the previous exercise, your professor has options on how to use this exercise. For example, s/he may assign you to be an associate to counsel for one of the parties and ask you to prepare a written or oral explanation whether this is sufficient to resist a summary judgment. Alternatively, s/he may have you argue the question before a magistrate judge. Finally, s/he may have you submit a short memo explaining to the magistrate judge how the judge should decide the original motion for summary judgment.

Here is the excerpt from the deposition that Ms. Connell has attached to her memorandum opposing the motion for summary judgment:

Q. Do you know Nathan Loewe?

A. You know the answer to that question.

Q. Mr. Ridge, please put your answer on the record.

A. Yes, I do know him.

Q. In fact, your phone records show that you have made phone calls to him over the past few years and your Rolodex includes his phone number, true?

A. Yes, that is true.

Q. Why did you call him, if not because you wanted information about the police raid?

A. Matters that don't involve this case.

Q. Specifically?

MR. RUSSELL: Objection. The question is not relevant to this dispute.

MS. CONNELL: Coop, I don't think that Judge Leach would want us to show up in his chambers again. Let's go off record and see if we can resolve this without me needing to file a motion to compel an answer.

(Resuming the deposition):

MS. CONNELL: As we agreed, you will answer my question. Do you need Ms. Webster to read it back to you?

A. No. I remember.

Q. Your answer?

A. I called him about another rumor about Judge Elliot.

Q. Specifically?

A. Whether he was having an affair.

# IV. CASES RELEVANT TO SECTION III. B

## LUNDEEN v. CORDNER

United States Court of Appeals Eighth Circuit, 1966

GIBSON, CIRCUIT JUDGE.

Appellant, plaintiff below, (hereinafter referred to as plaintiff) is a former wife of one Joseph Cordner, deceased. During their marriage two children were born, Maureen Joan Cordner and Michael Joseph Cordner. Prior to the time of his death Joseph Cordner was working in Libya. Mr. Cordner's employer Socony Mobil Oil Company, Inc. (Socony) carried a group life insurance contract with Metropolitan Life Insurance Company, (Metropolitan) under which Mr. Cordner as the insured had in 1956 designated his children, Maureen and Michael, as equal beneficiaries. In 1958 Joseph Cordner, having been divorced by plaintiff, married intervener, France Jeanne Cordner. In April 1960 a child was born of this second marriage. On October 3, 1962 Joseph Cordner died. During all periods above mentioned Mr. Cordner was in the employ of Socony stationed in Libya. The insurance policy and the annuity were in effect and due proof of loss was made. The contest for the proceeds arises between adverse claimants; the original designated beneficiaries, Maureen Joan and Michael Joseph Cordner; and France Jeanne Cordner, the second wife of assured, and Northwestern, as Trustee under the Last Will and Testament of Joseph F. Cordner, deceased.

On November 5, 1963, plaintiff as guardian and on behalf of her two children Maureen and Michael Cordner, the named beneficaries, sued the insurer, Metropolitan, to recover the proceeds of the policy. Metropolitan answered that there were adverse claims to the policy benefits. Thereafter, Northwestern as the Trustee under the Last Will and Testament of the deceased, Joseph Cordner, was interpleaded as an additional defendant. Appellee, France J. Cordner, then intervened in the action. Both intervener and Northwestern allege that sometime in 1961 the decedent effected a change of beneficiaries [in favor of the intervener]. * * *

It is clear that the first two children of decedent, Maureen and Michael, are the named beneficiaries. However, it is asserted that Joseph Cordner did everything within his power to effect a change of beneficiaries as alleged by intervener. Intervener presented affidavits and exhibits in support of her position and moved for summary judgment. The motion was granted and plaintiff contests this ruling on the ground that a summary judgment is not proper at this point in the litigation and that there remains a genuine issue on a material fact. It is now our task to determine if the summary judgment was properly granted.

* * * Plaintiff accepts as controlling the general rule of law that an insured's attempt to change his beneficiary will be given effect if all that remains to be done is a ministerial duty on the part of the insurer. * * *

Therefore, if deceased completed all the necessary steps required of him to change the beneficiary in his policy, intervener would be entitled to judgment. Furthermore, if intervener can demonstrate this fact so clearly that there is no longer a genuine issue of fact, summary judgment may be properly granted under provisions of Rule 56(c) of the Fed.R.Civ.P. * * *

We are of the opinion that the affidavits and exhibits introduced by intervener clearly and undeniably indicate that deceased made a change in his policy's beneficiaries. First, it appears that after deceased's marriage in 1958 to intervener he amended his group hospitalization and employee savings plan to include intervener. Furthermore, certain correspondence conclusively indicates that a change in the life insurance was actually made.

Mr. Iten, an employee of Socony in Libya, whose duties included administration of company benefit plans, advising employees concerning the plans, referring questions about the plans to the New York office, issuing change of beneficiary forms on request, and offering necessary guidance on completion and execution of forms, (after consultation with the deceased in April 1961) prepared a letter to the New York office, dated April 19, 1961, stating that Joseph Cordner desired information as to who were his present beneficiaries under the company benefit plans and that Mr. Cordner had married for a second time and was not certain whether he had changed his beneficiary. This letter from the Libyan office was answered under date of May 3, 1961 informing him that his designated beneficiaries were Maureen Joan Cordner, 50 per cent, and Michael Joseph Cordner, 50 per cent; the letter further gratuitously asking whether he would prefer the entire benefit to be paid to any survivor in the event of the death of any of the named beneficiaries.

Mr. Iten was transferred from Libya shortly thereafter and his duties were assumed by Mr. Burks. Burks by affidavit stated that early in 1961 Mr. Cordner came to him with a request to change his beneficiaries; that Burks issued the necessary forms to Cordner and gave him instructions on how to complete the forms, at which time Cordner produced a copy of his Will made in North Dakota while vacationing from Libya in 1960. They discussed the form of beneficiary designation which might be appropriate under the terms of the Will. Mr. Cordner personally completed the forms, endorsed the beneficiary changes he wished to make on the back of each form, signed the forms in Burks' presence, (the latter acting as a witness to the signature) and then left the completed forms with Burks for transmittal. Since Burks was unfamiliar with the type of beneficiary changes endorsed on the forms he made a thermofax copy of Cordner's Will and sent this reproduction together with the completed change of beneficiary forms to the New York office in a letter dated May 11, 1961, which letter in part reads as follows:

'Please review the enclosed employee change of beneficiary forms and advise us if this designation is acceptable under the plan.'

The Home Office responded by stating in a letter dated June 1, 1961:

> 'We are processing the Change of Beneficiary forms completed by the above employee (J. F. Cordner) and forwarded to us. * * * We see no reason why the designation will not be acceptable.'

Mr. Burks in his earlier affidavit of March 30, 1963 states that to the best of his recollection the change of beneficiary requested by Cordner was as follows:

> "One-fourth of the proceeds to my wife France Jeanne Cordner and the balance to the Northwestern National Bank of Minneapolis, Minneapolis, Minnesota in trust for the uses and purposes set forth in my Last Will and Testament."

Burks in his second affidavit prepared for the purpose of the summary judgment proceeding confirmed the factual statements in his earlier affidavit and detailed the discussion and the procedures employed in the requested change of beneficiary by Cordner. He further stated that since the New York office had the Certificate for endorsement and since the Home Office stated in its letter of June 1, 1961 that they were processing the change of beneficiary forms he had no reason to believe that the processing of the changes had not proceeded to completion in the normal course. He was in the New York office at the time when a search of the files was made for the change of beneficiary forms, which, of course, they were unable to locate. When he returned to Tripoli, with instructions from the New York office to continue the search and to forward to New York all company papers having to do with Mr. Cordner's employment, he found a copy of a letter addressed to Cordner by his attorney suggesting the form of beneficiary designation required to effect the provisions of his Will. Burks then recalled that Mr. Cordner had referred to this same letter when discussing beneficiary changes in 1961 and that Cordner had used the suggested language in completing his change of beneficiary forms. After stating that he cannot restate from memory the text of the changes, he said that 'I can and do reconfirm, upon my own direct knowledge and positive recollection that beneficiary changes so made by Joseph Franklin Cordner were in the form suggested by his attorney's letter and quoted verbatim from that letter in my prior affidavit.'

Further correspondence indicates that the change of beneficiary forms were forwarded to the employer's Annuity and Insurance Department. A search of the department, however, never uncovered the form or the exact language used therein. It also appears by affidavit that all of the above related correspondence was properly identified and was prepared, mailed, received and kept as part of the business records of the company.

Plaintiff presents no counter evidence nor in any way indicates that intervener's evidence is not worthy of belief. Therefore, we believe there is no genuine issue of fact on this point. It is clear that Joseph Cordner actually made a change in the beneficiaries of his life insurance policy.

However, to entitle intervener to summary judgment, it must not only be clear that a change was made, but the wording of that change must be shown beyond any reasonable and genuine dispute. This point, too, was well covered in intervener's supporting papers.

* * *

From the affidavit of the attorney concerning the discussion of deceased's desires, from the letter written by the attorney explaining how the beneficiaries should be changed to effectuate these desires, and from the wording of the Last Will and Testament it is clear that Joseph Cordner intended to change the beneficiaries of his insurance policy by giving one-fourth to intervener and the balance to Northwestern in trust. We can presume that this intent remained with Mr. Cordner during the intervening ten months between the Will's execution and the date of the beneficiary change. This presumption is supported by the presence of his unrevoked Will, which in itself indicates that he maintained this intent even until the time of his death, a year and a half after the change in beneficiary was sent to the company's home office. When we take this information along with the proof that some sort of beneficiary change was actually made by Mr. Cordner, and that the only change discovered was set out in Mr. Traynor's letter, we can presume that the change was made in accordance with this expressed intent. Otherwise, this unrevoked provision in Mr. Cordner's Will would have no force or effect.

However, in addition to this presumption we have the uncontested affidavits of a non-interested third party who was in a position to be aware of the actual wording of the change. The affiant, Mr. Harold Burks, was a fellow employee of Mr. Cordner in Libya, and supervised Mr. Cordner in filling out the required change of beneficiary forms. Mr. Burks is probably the only person that was in a position to be aware of the wording of the document. His affidavits are entitled to considerable weight in determining the merits of a summary judgment motion, especially where there is no indication of any counter-evidence. Moreover, Mr. Burks' assistance in processing the change in beneficiary was done in the regular course of business of Socony, and pursuant to his assigned duties. It has been held that the clear affidavits from the only persons in a position to be aware of a factual situation can well serve as the basis for a summary judgment. Dyer v. MacDougall, 201 F.2d 265 (2 Cir. 1952).

* * *

So, in support of intervener's claim there is undisputed proof that Mr. Cordner had manifested an intent to give intervener one-fourth of his insurance proceeds with the balance going into the trust established by his Will. It is likewise clear beyond any shadow of doubt that Mr. Cordner subsequently made a change in his insurance beneficiaries. The logical conclusion is clear. He made the change in accordance with his prior expressed intent. This presumption is supported by the two affidavits of Mr. Burks which recite from direct and positive recollection that the beneficiary changes were copied from Mr. Cordner's letter from his attorney and were in form exactly as alleged by intervener.

In response to the overwhelming documentary evidence supported by affidavits all of which consistently showed that Cordner had requested a change of beneficiary in accordance with his lawyer's letter and his own Last Will and Testament, the plaintiff submitted her own counter-affidavit to the effect that Mr. Cordner was very much interested in the welfare of his first two children (the named beneficiaries) and was aware of the future financial difficulties they would face. No further information was offered. The Court, therefore, was not presented with a situation where it was asked to weigh conflicting affidavits. The problem was only, did the affidavits and exhibits of intervener sustain the necessary burden in order to allow a summary judgment? The trial court felt the burden was sustained, and from the above related facts we agree with the trial court's conclusion. The showing made by intervener on the motion for summary judgment covers all of the material issues of fact in the case and as found by the trial judge, Cordner had 'effectively changed the beneficiaries in his group policy and that he did all that he was required to do.'

We are of the opinion that if this information were presented at trial, intervener would be entitled to a directed verdict in her favor, and it has been said that if the information presented entitles one to a directed verdict, a summary judgment is in order. * * * Intervener having made a sufficient showing, it then rests upon the plaintiff to specify at least some evidence which could be produced at trial. * * * Plaintiff apparently is of the opinion that, since she makes a prima facie case by merely introducing the Certificate showing her children as designated beneficiaries, she is entitled to a trial on the issue of (1) whether any change of beneficiary was made, and (2) if so, what changes were actually made. This we do not feel is a correct view of the law.

The counter-affidavit of the plaintiff does not meet the issues raised and supported by the intervener. This leaves no genuine issue as to any material fact, and presents a predicate for a summary judgment under Rule 56(c), Fed.R.Civ.P.

* * *

The real gravamen of plaintiff's objection is not that there is conflicting evidence but rather that the summary judgment rests upon the affidavits of Harold Burks. His testimony being so vital to intervener's cause, it is asserted that the case should proceed to trial in order that the demeanor of the witness could be observed and his testimony subjected to the test of cross-examination.

In passing on this contention it might be well to make four preliminary observations. First, affiant Burks appears to be an unbiased witness. He has no financial or personal interest in the outcome of this litigation. Second, there is no doubt but what his testimony is competent both in regard to his mental capacity and his being in a position to directly observe the facts related in his affidavits. Third, his participation in the change of beneficiaries was in the regular course of his duties with Socony. Finally, both affidavits are positive, internally consistent, unequivocal, and in full accord with the documentary exhibits. Therefore, even though cross-examination is a trial right which must be carefully protected, in this case, unlike many others there is no obvious advantage to be gained from a cross-examination. If there were, a summary judgment might arguably be improper. But where there is no indication that the affiant was biased, dishonest, mistaken, unaware or unsure of the facts, the cases declaring that cross-examination is necessary when one of the above is present, have no application here. There being no positive showing that this witness's testimony could be impeached or that he might have additional testimony valuable to plaintiff, summary judgment was properly granted. The opposing party cannot as a matter of course force a trial merely in order to cross-examine such an affiant, nor must the Court deny the motion for summary judgment on the basis of a vague supposition that something might turn up at the trial. * * *

There is absolutely no showing that a trial would produce any different or additional evidence. It appears that Burks is now stationed in Singapore, far beyond the subpoena powers of the trial court. Neither party would be able to compel his attendance before the trial court. Since this witness is out of the jurisdiction, any of the parties, on the other hand, would be free to introduce Burks' testimony by use of a deposition. Therefore, in all likelihood Burks would never have to appear in open court. What would plaintiff have to gain by forcing a trial under these circumstances? We feel very little, if anything. A full trial would not give plaintiff an opportunity to cross-examine Burks in open court, nor would it unveil his demeanor to the trier of fact.

In the event of a trial plaintiff would only be free to obtain Burks' sworn testimony by deposition or upon written interrogatories pursuant to Rule 28(b) or Rule 31, Fed.R.Civ.P. and by 28 U.S.C.A. § 1783(a)(1). Plaintiff, however, was free to take this action even prior to the present motion for summary judgment but chose not to do so. When the motion for summary judgment was presented, plaintiff, if she felt Burks had information valuable to her cause, was again free to move for a delay in judgment and secure Burks' deposition. Again plaintiff took no action. Apparently plaintiff felt she had nothing to gain by a deposition, yet under the circumstances of this case that is probably the most she could expect even if this case went to trial. Therefore, we do not feel that plaintiff is in a position at this time to force a trial. A trial would not secure Burks' presence, it would only force the taking of his deposition, a course previously open to plaintiff which she elected not to pursue.

* * *

The position declaring that a party opposed to a summary judgment based upon affidavits must assume some initiative in showing that a factual issue actually exists is perfectly sound in the light of Rule 56, Fed.R.Civ.P., which specifically allows the use of affidavits in summary judgment proceedings. For if plaintiff's position is correct that an affiant's credibility is always an issue for the trial court, then the granting of a summary judgment would be virtually impossible when it is based in any way upon an affidavit. Rule 56 would be nullified by the prevailing party's use of one affidavit and the bald objection by the opposing party to the affiant's credibility. The reference in this rule to 'affidavits' would therefore be of no effect.

This does not mean that an affiant's credibility cannot properly be put in issue by a litigant, but in doing so specific facts must be properly produced. At this point the 1963 amendment to Rule 56(e) comes into play requiring the opposing party to respond or suffer the fate of a summary judgment, if otherwise appropriate. Plaintiff failed to respond to the adequate and substantial showing of intervener, so the trial court properly granted the summary judgment. Keeping in mind that the purpose of the summary judgment is to avoid useless trials, from the circumstances of this case we believe a trial would indeed be a useless waste of time and expense to the parties as well as a needless inconvenience to the Court.

* * *

Judgment affirmed.

## CROSS v. UNITED STATES OF AMERICA

United States Court of Appeals Second Circuit
1964

MOORE, CIRCUIT JUDGE:

In this income tax refund suit, plaintiffs-appellees claim that they were entitled to a deduction of $1,300 on their joint return for the year 1954 because of expenses incurred by Professor Ephraim Cross in connection with his summer travel to various Mediterranean and European countries. Upon appellees' motion for summary judgment, the district court, whose examination of the facts included the affidavits of several professors tending to indicate the desirability of foreign travel for a teacher of languages as well as the pre-trial deposition of Professor Cross, concluded that there was no genuine issue as to any material fact, and granted appellees' motion. * * * The Government opposed the summary judgment procedure, claiming a right to cross-examine appellees as to the nature of their expenses and the educational benefits allegedly sought and also to cross-examine the affiant professors. On this appeal the only issue is whether there are triable issues of fact which render the award of summary judgment erroneous.

In 1954 Professor Cross was an Assistant Professor at City College in New York where he taught French, Spanish and romance linguistics (described by him as the study of the development of Latin into the romance languages, the study of the various dialects and the historic stages of those dialects). He, his wife and a pet dog sailed from New York on June 30, 1954 aboard a French freighter. The ship put in briefly in Portugal, Morocco, Tangiers, Oran, Algiers, Naples and Genoa and appellees spent a day or so in each place. When the freighter arrived at Marseilles, twenty-one days after leaving New York, appellees separated. Mrs. Cross joined a friend and continued touring while Professor Cross and their pet dog travelled to Paris. Although he did not pursue a formal course of study or engage in research, Professor Cross did visit schools, courts of law, churches, book publishers, theaters, motion pictures, restaurants, cafes and other places of amusement, read newspapers, listen to radio broadcasts, converse with students and teachers and attend political meetings. He rejoined his wife in this country on September 23, 1954 after his return aboard a French passenger liner.

Section 162(a), Int.Rev.Code of 1954 permits a deduction for 'all the ordinary and necessary expenses paid or incurred * * * in carrying on any trade or business * * *.' The Regulations promulgated under that section, Treas. Reg. 1.162–5, state:

'Expenses for education—(a) Expenditures made by a taxpayer for his education are deductible if they are for education (including research activities) undertaken primarily for the purpose of:

'(1) Maintaining or improving skills required by the taxpayer in his employment or trade or business,

* * * * * *

'Whether or not education is of the type referred to in subparagraph (1) of this paragraph shall be determined upon the basis of all the facts of each case. If it is customary for other established members of the taxpayer's trade or business to undertake such education, the taxpayer will ordinarily be considered to have undertaken this education for the purposes described in subparagraph (1) of this paragraph.

* * * * * *

'(c) In general, a taxpayer's expenditures for travel (including travel while on sabbatical leave) as a form of education shall be considered as primarily personal in nature and therefore not deductible.'

Appellees claim, and the district court held, that all of Professor Cross's expenses are deductible. Professor Cross asserted in his deposition, which was taken for discovery purposes and did not include cross-examination,

'My purpose (in making the trip) was to maintain my contacts with my foreign languages for the purpose of maintaining and improving my skill as a linguist and teacher of languages, and to make my general teaching more effective, and to extend my contacts with foreign culture which I have to teach in connection with my teaching of foreign languages per se, and this can be done effectively and properly only by going into a foreign language area.'

The Government disputes this explanation. It contends that all or at least part of Professor Cross's travel was a vacation and thus a personal living expense for which a deduction is not allowed under Section 162, Int.Rev.Code of 1954. Moreover, the Government challenges the amount of the claimed deduction and questions whether any portion of that sum was expended on behalf of Mrs. Cross.

We believe that summary judgment was improvidently granted and that the Government is entitled to a trial at which all the circumstances may be developed for the consideration of the trier of fact. Rule 56(c), Fed.R.Civ.P. permits summary judgment only where 'there is no genuine issue as to any material fact,' a state of affairs not normally encountered where the problem is whether expenses are ordinary and necessary in carrying on a taxpayer's trade or business. * * * Before travelling expenses can be allowed as deductible, there must be a factual determination of what parts, if any, are to be attributed to vacation travel or to educational advancement.

The essentially factual character of the issue is particularly apparent here, where the ultimate facts were warmly contested. While there was no dispute that Professor Cross was a teacher of languages and that he travelled abroad, many of the facts remain largely within his own knowledge and the Government should have the opportunity to test his credibility on cross-examination. Summary judgment is particularly inappropriate where 'the inferences which the parties seek to have drawn deal with questions of motive, intent and subjective feelings and reactions.' * * * "A judge may not, on a motion for summary judgment, draw fact inferences. * * * Such inferences may be drawn only on a trial." * * * While we have recently emphasized that ordinarily the bare allegations of the pleadings, unsupported by specific evidentiary data, will not alone defeat a motion for summary judgment, * * * this principle does not justify summary relief where, as here, the disputed questions of fact turn exclusively on the credibility of movants' witnesses.

To the teacher of modern languages, particularly in a country far removed from the European continent, it is highly important that his linguistic ear be retuned as frequently as possible to the ways in which a foreign language is expressed. Moreover, a thorough familiarity with the current social, political and cultural climate of a country properly may be regarded as a prerequisite to effective classroom presentation of its language. * * *

On the other hand, a mere pleasure trip through various countries by a professor who has some fluency with the language of each country might well not fall within the deductible category. * * *

Who can doubt that the alert American trial lawyer as a part of a summer vacation might not profit greatly by spending some time at the Old Bailey listening to British barristers exhibit their skills. The surgeon, too, might be benefitted in his profession by observing some delicate operation conducted by a European surgeon of renown. Yet it is questionable whether such tangible evidences of constant interest in one's profession entitle a taxpayer to deduct all his summer vacation expenses.

In addition to determining whether the trip was devoted in whole or in part to educational advancement, the trier of the facts will have to ascertain such amounts as are to be attributed to such purpose. Were the preliminary twenty-one days prior to the Marseilles landing all part of an educational program? What part, if any, was allocable to Mrs. Cross? What charges were incurred by the dog? Although probably de minimis, the Treasury frequently watches every penny and might not be generously inclined even though the dog were a French poodle.

The district court reasoned that summary judgment should be granted because the Government did not adduce facts to refute Professor Cross's claims as to the purpose of his trip, and that the Government had an opportunity to cross-examine when taking his deposition. The 'right to use depositions for discovery * * * does not mean that they are to supplant the right to call and examine the adverse party * * * before the jury. * * * 'We cannot very well overestimate the importance of having the witness examined and cross-examined in presence of the court and jury." * * * By the same process, Professor Cross will have an opportunity to show with greater particularity that his more modern approach to the problem of linguistic improvement is far superior to the old-fashioned classroom lecture method.

Reversed and remanded for trial.

## DYER v. MacDOUGALL

United States Court of Appeals Second Circuit, 1952
201 F.2d 265

Before SWAN, CHIEF JUDGE, and L. HAND and FRANK, CIRCUIT JUDGES.

L. HAND, CIRCUIT JUDGE.

This case comes up on appeal by the plaintiff from a judgment summarily dismissing the third * * * count[] of a complaint for * * * slander. [Defendant presented the trial court with affidavits of all of the persons present when defendant was supposed to have made the defamatory statements; all of them denied plaintiff's allegations.]

* * * if the cause went to trial, the plaintiff would have no witnesses by whom he could prove the slanders alleged in the third and fourth counts, except the two defendants, * * *; and they would all deny that the slanders had been uttered. On such a showing how could he escape a directed verdict? It is true that the carriage, behavior, bearing, manner and appearance of a witness—in short, his 'demeanor'—is a part of the evidence. The words used are by no means all that we rely on in making up our minds about the truth of a question that arises in our ordinary affairs, and it is abundantly settled that a jury is as little confined to them as we are. They may, and indeed they should, take into consideration the whole nexus of sense impressions which they get from a witness. This we have again and again declared, and have rested our affirmance of findings of fact of a judge, or of a jury, on the hypothesis that this part of the evidence may have turned the scale. Moreover, such evidence may satisfy the tribunal, not only that the witness' testimony is not true, but that the truth is the opposite of his story; for the denial of one, who has a motive to deny, may be uttered with such hesitation, discomfort, arrogance or defiance, as to give assurance that he is fabricating, and that, if he is, there is no alternative but to assume the truth of what he denies.

Nevertheless, although it is therefore true that in strict theory a party having the affirmative might succeed in convincing a jury of the truth of his allegations in spite of the fact that all the witnesses denied them, we think it plain that a verdict would nevertheless have to be directed against him. This is owing to the fact that otherwise in such cases there could not be an effective appeal from the judge's disposition of a motion for a directed verdict. He, who has seen and heard the 'demeanor' evidence, may have been right or wrong in thinking that it gave rational support to a verdict; yet, since that evidence has disappeared, it will be impossible for an appellate court to say which he was. Thus, he would become the final arbiter in all cases where the evidence of witnesses present in court might be determinative. * * *

[The court affirmed the lower court's judgment.]

†